A LINE IN THE SAND

Saudi Arabia's Role in the Gulf War

SULAYMAN NYANG
&
EVAN HENDRICKS

Cover by Carlos Arrien

P.T. BOOKS
1995

ISBN: 0-9645486-0-7
First Edition

FOREWORD

The Gulf War of 1991 was truly an epochal event of the twentieth century. Although it arose from a regional base it clearly had global influence. It overturned certain fundamental assumptions about the relationship of nations and especially the relationship of states within the *Ummah* (Commonwealth of Muslim Nations) and established new equations for these relationships. It is probable, though not yet certain, that, granted moderate oscillations characteristic of all epochal change, these new relationships are irreversible. There is not likely to be a return to the *status quo ante*.

The critical factor in activating the response to Iraq's invasion of the sovereign State of Kuwait was the correctly perceived threat to the territorial integrity of Saudi Arabia. The response of King Fahd to the mission led by U.S. Secretary of Defense Richard Cheney was unequivocal and immediate. Indeed it was remarkable in view of earlier refusals to allow establishment of U.S. bases in the Kingdom. The obvious reason for such a reaction by King Fahd was the double threat to oil wealth and to national sovereignty. But the Islamic context of the decision and the conflict must also be considered. The authors of this book quite wisely devote 16 pages (Chapter 8) to this dimension. The religious fabric can never be detached from analysis of Muslim nations. This is truer for Saudi Arabia than for any other Muslim state. The Kingdom is the only Muslim state whose constitution is the Holy Qur'an and whose polity is the *Shariah* (Islamic Law). Moreover, Saudi Arabia geographically embraces the holy cities of Makkah and Medina, to which some two million pilgrims annually make the *hajj* and hundreds of thousands more make *umrah* (the minor pilgrimage) throughout the year. It is to Makkah that all Muslims turn in performing their obligatory prayers five times a day. Saudia Airlines have compasses on the ceilings of their cabins showing the direction of Makkah. It is not without significance that in October 1986 King Fahd decreed that the title "His Majesty" be replaced by the designation "Khadim al-Haramain al-Sharifain." This has been translated in the press and in official announcements as "Servant of the Two Holy Harams" and as "Custodian of the Two Holy Mosques." This is a reminder of the responsibility which the Kingdom bears to a global Islam now constituting 27 percent of the world's population. This responsibility bears on the consequent distinctive nature of the Saudi polity and on its status among other Muslim states. No other nation in the world so proudly relates its religious feeling with all aspects of life. Saudi Arabia is the only nation which has on its national flag the first of the Five Pillars of the Faith: "There is no god but Allah and Muhammed is His Prophet."

This Islamic idiom was of paramount significance in the Gulf War. The possibility of invasion of the Kingdom by Iraq and hence control of the Holy Places by a predominantly Shiite country, albeit governed by a Sunni Baathist regime, was horrible to contemplate. An unspoken, subliminal fear was the decision of King Hussain of the Hashemite Kingdom of Jordan to ally, along with Yemen and the PLO, on the side of Iraq. The politically obvious reason for this was Palestinian influence (slightly more than half of the population) in Jordan. This possible threat from Jordan was made more alarming by Yemen's siding with Iraq and Jordan. The perception was that a pincer movement - seizing the Eastern province (al-Hasa) where the oil wealth is located from bases in Kuwait, overrunning the Emirates in the south and allowing the Yemenis to take the Saudi southern province of Asir - would make the Saudi position untenable.

But a widely perceived fear was the possibility of

a secret understanding between Iraq's Saddam Hussein and King Hussain of Jordan to let the latter reclaim jurisdiction over the holy places of Makkah and Medina - jurisdiction once held by Sherif Hussein ibn Ali, great grandfather of King Hussein. It is unlikely that any country other than Saudi Arabia could discharge its responsibilities for the Holy Land with such munificence and efficiency. The refurbishing of the mosques, the world's largest air conditioning system built by Carrier, the tunnels, roads, health and sanitation facilities, ocean port and airport facilities in Jeddah, all have been a modern miracle of planning and mega-engineering.

Another threat rooted in the Islamic idiom was the possible violation of the sanctity of the holy places by non-Muslim troops of the United States and its allies. It was embarrassing enough that the Kingdom had to be protected by non-Muslim forces. Would these forces once in place respect the inviolate quality of the holy places which forbid entrance by non-Muslims? Whatever fears lurked in the minds of Saudi Arabia was quickly allayed first by the promises of American authorities and subsequently by the impeccable behavior of American and allied forces and by their quick withdrawal at the conflict's end. The sensitivities to the Muslim dimensions of the issue of a foreign presence were further evident in the polite Saudi refusal to allow American bases of personnel on Saudi soil. There was no objection to such bases in Kuwait or elsewhere in the Gulf or to pre-positioning of material in the Kingdom.

The American and allied forces were astounded by the efficiency of the Saudi logistical support as well as by the scope and physical dimensions of the infrastructure for deployment of troops and equipment. Had they compared Saudi Arabian development with that of other countries, they would not have been surprised. The accomplishments of the Kingdom surpass in magnitude and quality those of any other nation starting from a non-technocratic, in this case from a poor desert economy. Telecommunications, super-highways, housing, sports facilities, hospitals, seven universities - all are evidence of wise planning and judicious allocation of resources. Anyone who has visited Saudi Arabia periodically from 1970 to 1994 would find it difficult not to use the term "developmental miracle." But the miraculous aspects lie in more than physical facilities. The development has occurred within the context of an Islamic polity.

The political system of Saudi Arabia, widely misunderstood in the West, is correctly interpreted in this volume. The analysis of how King Fahd made the decision to allow American forces in the Kingdom is revealing. There was an extensive consultation process, institutionally different from that of the United States, but functionally equivalent. In the evolution of modern political systems there should be a sequence in the development process, building institutions first and then gradually allowing for an increase in popular demands. This is precisely what happened in the evolution of the American political system over a long period from 1620 through direct election of representatives to womens' suffrage and equal voting rights for all. It has not occurred in most developing countries where the extension of the political process to the periphery of the social order has exerted unbearable pressures on weak institutions. In the most extreme cases, as in frantic PLO efforts to establish governance in Gaza and Jericho, institutions do not exist. In Saudi Arabia the sequence of emphases in this developmental syndrome has been different from most systems. An institutional infrastructure was built before mass participation produced an escalation of demands incapable of being met. The sophistication and quality of this infrastructure, which so impressed American forces, was made possible only because of this sequence.

This gradualist approach to political development took a significant forward step when King Fahd announced in March 1992 the appointment of a national consultative council (*Majlis al-Shoura*). This was followed in August 1993 by the appointment of the Council's sixty members and a new cabinet system limiting cabinet terms of office. A new local government structure was announced in September 1993. Of some interest is the fact that of the 60 members of the Consultative Council, 31 hold doctorates from western (mostly American) universities. This is evidence of the close relationship between the Kingdom and the United States over many years and further evidence that the Gulf War certainly did nothing to put that relationship in jeopardy.

The response of Muslim states is dealt with admirably in this volume. It must, however, be placed in the context of global Muslim unity (or disunity). Deeply ingrained in the Muslim psyche is the context of the unity of all Muslims (*Ummah*). Once this unity had at least superficial recognition in the institution of the Sultan at Constantinople who was also the Caliph of global Islam. For centuries little more than a symbol, the Caliphate was abolished by Mustafa Kemal, father of modern Turkey, in March 1924. The strength of the symbolism was evident in the Khalifa movement in India, condemning the abolition of the Califate (Khalifa). As a mark of solidarity with Turkish Muslims, Indian Muslims took to wearing the Turkish faz, still worn by older devout Muslims in India and Pakistan.

After the abolition of the Califate under global decolonization which started in earnest after World War II, a unified Muslim movement was hindered by the colonial powers of Britain, France, Italy, and the Netherlands who governed most of the Islamic world. The first institutional reassertion of Muslim unity was establishment of the League of Arab States in Tunis in

1944 with Egypt, Iraq, Syria, Lebanon, and Saudi Arabia, and Transjordan (now Jordan) as charter members. The membership now consists of twenty-two states - all Arab. This sense of Arab solidarity was pushed forward by the pan-Arab movement of Egypt's Gamal Abdul Nasser as early as 1955, provoked further by the Suez War of 1956. This movement was a mini-*Ummah* limited to Arab states whose population was a minority of the Muslim world. We can call this the *Ummah Arabiya* in contrast to the all embracing *Ummah Islamiya*, both of which are important in contextualizing the analysis of the Gulf War in this volume. The pan-Arab movement was directed primarily against Zionism, imperialism, and feudalism. It took a step toward political unity by forming with Syria in 1958 the United Arab Republic (UAR). A few months later the Emir of Yemen joined the UAR in a federated entity labelled the United Arab States. This attempt at Arab unity was short lived. A military coup in Syria in 1961 forced withdrawal from the UAR. A few months later Egypt ousted Yemen. In 1964 Iraq and Egypt issued a proclamation to establish an Arab Socialist Union. There were similar Egyptian efforts to federate with the Sudan, Jordan, and in 1973 with Libya. None of these pan-Arab overtures materialized.

Nevertheless the fantasy of an Arab nation persists in the Arab psyche. It was evident in the Gulf War by assertions that the invasion of Kuwait was an Arab problem which should be resolved exclusively by Arabs. In fact the Gulf War probably discounted for sometime to come the myth of Arab unity. The Arab nation of Iraq violated its commitment to Saudi Arabia, invaded a sovereign Arab state and threatened others. In consequence the Saudi attitude towards Iraq, Yemen, Jordan, and the Palestinians was drastically altered. The myth of *Ummah Islamiya*, embracing some one billion Muslims was not diminished and may have been enhanced by the Gulf War. This concept was first given a structure by King Faisal of Saudi Arabia in establishing the Organization of the Islamic Conference (OIC) in Jeddah in 1971. Even before the OIC, Saudi Arabia had created the World Muslim League (Rabitat al-Alam al Islamia) as a quasi-official entity to unite religious cultural, youth, welfare, and public service organizations, both national and international throughout the Muslim world. Its annual meetings are attended by representatives of some 200 Muslim organizations. The OIC has eclipsed the League of Arab States in many ways. Consisting of 46 member states, the secretariat in Jeddah has more than 120 staff members appointed from throughout the Muslim world. Its annual meetings of foreign ministers, and usually triannial summits of heads of state, have dealt with pressing issues - reconciliation of Pakistan and Bangladesh, Jerusalem policy, Afghanistan, the Iran-Iraq War, and many others.

The Gulf Cooperation Council, established in 1981, is made up of the six states of the Arabian peninsula: the United Arab Emirates, Bahrain, Saudi Arabia, Oman, Qatar, and Kuwait. It is a dynamic and highly effective organization, limited to the "New Arabians" who share, more than any other Arab grouping, common geography, resources, culture, and strategic interests.

The four entities - the League of Arab States, the Rabitat al-Alam al-Islamia, the Organization of the Islamic Conference, and the Gulf Cooperation, form a network of Islamic and Arab solidarity. That solidarity is disturbed from time to time. Egypt was expelled from the League by signing the Camp David agreement and the League headquarters was moved to Tunis. But Egypt has been readmitted and the secretariat is once again in Cairo, while other fissures involving Jordan, Iraq, Yemen, and the PLO occur periodically. The significant fact is that all of these organizations supported the Gulf War. The concept of global Arab unity was weakened by the war but ironically, the institutional structure, though diminished in scope, was strengthened by the unanimity of the larger universe of Muslim states siding with Saudi Arabia and Kuwait.

Ralph Braibanti
James B. Duke Professor of
Political Science Emeritus
Duke University
Debember 1994

CONTENTS

FOREWORD

ABOUT THE AUTHORS

1

IRAQ AND KUWAIT: HISTORICAL SETTING

The Gulf War, which was one of the major events of 1991, was the result of the conflict between the Republic of Iraq and the State of Kuwait. The invasion of the latter by the leader of the former set the stage for the great showdown that has entered the history books as the Gulf War or, to borrow the name given to this tragedy by its initial perpetrator, President Saddam Hussein of Iraq, the "Mother of all wars." Whether it was the "mother of all wars" or the beginning of the end of President Saddam Hussein only history would tell. In the remaining pages of this chapter, it is the intention of the authors to look at the history of the area and then discuss the background to the conflict. This is done with the understanding that the observer of events in the area cannot really understand what is going on in the area unless and until he or she comes to grip with the history and culture of the peoples of Iraq and Kuwait. It is to this and other related questions that we now turn.

The republic we now call Iraq has a long history compared to many other Arab states. Its roots go back to antiquity. Like ancient Egypt where the Nile facilitated the emergence of an agrarian civilization, Iraq also is a country where two rivers, the Euphrates and the Tigris "allowed the early development of a complex irrigated agriculture. With increased food supply came population growth and the rise of the earliest cities."[1] Such cities were the results of the vocational specialization among the ancient Iraqis. The creation of a leisure class enabled the ancient society to make significant strides forward. Evidences of this significant transformation were the wheel, the plow, metallurgy, massive architecture, writing, mathematics, complex government, and written codes of law. The civilizations we now know as Sumerian and Babylonian were the earliest urban manifestations of the human spirit acting itself out in the bosom of the twin rivers.

What is particularly striking about the Mesopotamian valley-plain is the fact that it has served as a major center of civilization for several millennia. The irrigation system developed by the earlier civilizations continued to serve the peoples of the area until the invasion of the region by the Mongols from central Asia in the thirteenth century. Iraqis who witnessed the destruction of their country in the Gulf War are likely to compare the damage done by American bombs with the massacres carried out by the Mongols when they acted upon the decision of their leader, Hulagu.

The coming of Islam to Iraq was destined to alter the course of history among the peoples of Iraq. Committed to a new way of looking at reality and determined to live by the Qu'ran, the Muslims who came as conquerors in Iraq and the peoples they found there soon evolved a culture and civilization that would wipe out much of the *jahiliyya* in their history and culture. Because of the unique history of Iraq, its peoples have come to be perceived differently from other Arabs. This uniqueness of the Iraqis has been debated among the scholars writing on Iraq. As one author puts it, these distinctions "are not easy to identify, much less to demonstrate, but few observers would deny that there are aspects of community life in Iraq and a characteristic approach to the problems of government, technology, and economic organization which in degree or kind set off the country from its Arab neighbors despite common Moslem (sic) traditions and faith, and a shared language."[2]

The historical transformations which took place in Iraq since the earlier days have not necessarily eliminated all traces of the ancient ways. There are two strategic reasons. First of all, the existence of a vast desert just miles away from the plains facing the two rivers created the opening for foreign armies and traders to penetrate the area. Secondly, the passes in the mountains to the north and east enabled those who wished to enter the area to come in without much difficulty. It was indeed these access points that the Sumerians, the Akkidians, the Babylonians, the Greeks, the Romans, the Arabs, the Mongols, and the Turks followed to conquer the ancestors of Saddam Hussein and his fellow countrymen and women. In retrospect, we can now say that it was the individual contributions of these peoples and their cultures that built the cultural foundations of modern day Iraq.

In our attempt to provide the historical background to the Gulf crisis we would be unsuccessful if we fail to show how the common history and destinies of the three important regional actors in the conflict are linked together by the Islamic movement that took the whole area some years after the death of the prophet Muhammad. It should be stated here that for at least 1400 years the peoples of this part of the Middle East have lived under the influence of the Islamic religion. Not only have the original languages in the area yielded to Arabic, but their native speakers are now so thoroughly Arabized that today they proudly assert their Arabness within the framework of the Arab League, the Organization of Islamic Conference, and the United Nations. The primacy of the Arab identity is largely due to the legacy of the Ottoman period and the deep-seated nature of Islam and Arabic in Iraqi life. Although there were many minorities at the time when the British colonial inheritors of the Arab remnants of the Ottoman Empire decided to give birth to this new country in the Middle East, the Jewish elements have virtually disappeared because of the hostilities that have developed between Israelis and Arabs since the creation of the Hebrew state some forty-three years ago. With the exception of the Kurds, no other linguistic or ethnic group has decided to stake its own independent claim to statehood. The Shiites of the south have always asserted their separate religious identity; however, because of their Arab identity, they have learned to co-exist with the Sunni neighbors. This reconciliation, however tentative it may appear to those of us from abroad, remains up until the eruption of the Gulf War, and the subsequent attempt of the Shiites to liberate their territories from the grip of the ruling Baath party of Saddam Hussein. In retrospect, we can argue that the Shiites seem to have worked out a *modus vivendi* with their Sunni Arab brethren. The Iran-Iraq War was a great test of loyalty to many Iraqis. Caught between the patriotic demands of the Iraqi state and the religious calls of the Khomeini forces in their sectarian neighborhood, many a Shiite chose Iraq over Iran. This selection process will be the bone of contention among academics for many years to come. But, regardless of how one may feel about this situation, the fact remains that Islam and the Arabic language will not only continue to capture the imagination of the average Iraqi, but they will for a long time determine the answers given by the Iraqi people to the following questions: (i) Who are you?; (ii) What are your identities and how do you relate to the other peoples of the Middle East? This quest for a distinct and unique Iraqi identity has only developed over the last sixty years, although one should quickly add that territorial identification with the land between the Tigris and the Euphrates within the old Ottoman Empire, gave meaning to the Iraqi sense of belonging. The development of pan-Arabism simply strengthened this consciousness and the Iraqi intellectuals and politicians have over the last sixty years managed to manipulate this aspect of the Iraqi life and culture. The invasion of Kuwait is justified, rightly or wrongly, on the basis of the Iraqi leadership's reading of human history in that part of the world.

The Historical Roots of Modern Iraq

As already pointed out, the history of modern Iraq goes back to ancient times. Historians usually tell us this history is at least over 3000 years. The beginnings of ancient Iraq made her contemporary to the First Egyptian Dynasty. Recorded history goes only back to the Sumerians. These mysterious civilization builders of Mesopotamia carried the torch of human civilization for many years before they disappeared in the black hole of the human past. They were replaced in turn by the Amorites, an ancient people who are believed to have migrated from Syria. Many dynasties were established by this group. The two most important centers of civilized life were Ninevah and Nimrod to the north of the river Tigris, and Babylon in the south on the river Euphrates. Babylon was famous because of its power and civilization. Historians tell us one of the earliest lawgivers, Hammurabi, hailed from this place. Ruling between 1792 to 1750 B.C., he introduced the celebrated body of laws now known as the Hammurabi Code. Indeed, the Babylonians extended their influence not only over portions of modern day Iraq, but also over parts of southern Turkey and a sizable part of modern day Syria. As an Amorite ruler, Hammurabi introduced a number of legal codes which address many problems of human life. Some of the problems addressed, such as land tenure, marriage, the position of women, the function of money and types of exchange contracts, public order and so on, are still relevant.

The Amorites soon lost power to a new force called the Assyrians. This new center of gravity brought a revolution in military warfare. It is generally agreed among scholars that the Assyrians were able to establish hegemony in the Middle East because of their invention of iron for war purposes. This new technology soon gave them advantages over their neighbors. They conquered Syria, Babylon, and Egypt. They introduced into human society for the first time the bureaucratization of military power. This new technique of managing power over defeated peoples served their purpose only for a while. In time their control was challenged and soon Egypt and Syria were lost. By 606 B.C. the great Assyrian empire collapsed and the power and glory associated with it disappeared from the stage of history. The conquerors who humbled the Assyrians were the Scythians. They destroyed Nineveh and sent their predecessors into the mighty trash bin of history. The only reminder to the Assyrian heritage are the modern day Iraqi Christians of the Nestorian sect who claim to be the ethnic descent from the dominant peoples of this ancient empire.

With the collapse of the Assyrians Babylon rose up,

phoenix-like, from the ashes of Middle Eastern history. This new Babylon was catapulted to glory and power through the efforts of Nebuchadnezzar, one of the greatest rulers of the ancient world. But, like all the ancient empires, this one too fell under the powerful blows of history. Defeated by Cyrus the Great, the Babylonian empire disappeared. An Archaemenian Persian and known to biblical scholars as the liberator of the children of Israel, who had earlier been enslaved by Nebuchadnezzar, Cyrus took power in 539 B.C. The defeat of the Babylonians by the armies of Cyrus has been interpreted differently by different Western and Middle Eastern scholars. Those of the European tendency have interpreted the rise of the people of Cyrus as the beginning of hegemony by the Indo-Europeans over the Semites. They usually sketched a series of stages, beginning with the conquest of the Medes, a people related to the people of Cyrus. This people called Medes had already conquered the Babylonians and brought Nineveh under their control. With the death of Cyrus, power fell into the hands of his son, Cambyses, a man of great skills and fortitude who extended the power of his dynasty into Asia Minor and to the Oxus River. Historians usually referred to this empire as the last and greatest ancient Mesopotamian empire. It was known for its toleration of other faiths and as previously pointed out, Cyrus is remembered today as the Persian ruler who let the children of Israel go.

During this period in history of the Middle East, the Greek peoples of the area were destined to interact with their eastern neighbors. This came about when Alexander the Great made his adventures into the east. Prior to this famous adventure into Persian territories, there were occasional forays and these are now a part of our historical record of the East-West interactions of the ancient world. Alexander of Macedonia did not only capture the heart of Greek culture but he also added to his increasing territorial trophies significant portions of the ancient Middle East. However, in retrospect, one could argue that his dream of a synthesis of eastern and western values crumbled after his death in Babylon in 323 B.C. His territories were soon parcelled out among his generals and he too faded into history as other empire builders of another age stepped into his shoes and governed those who had earlier kowtowed to his commands. The Iraqis and Syrians of those days felt under the control of Seleucus, who founded a new capital named after himself. But as these Greek followers of Alexander struggled with the delicate tasks of governing this part of the Middle East, two new centers of gravity were developing. One was Rome to the West and the other was Persia under the Parthians. 185 years after the demise of Alexander, the remnants of his conquered empire to the east fell into the hands of the Parthian Persians. These new conquerors were destined by history to engage in an ongoing struggle between themselves and the Romans. This was to last until the Arabs swept out of Arabia under the banner of Islam.

It was indeed the triumph of the Islamic armies that put an end to the 800 years of fighting between Byzantines and Persians. The history of the region was changed for good by the victories of the Muslim armies. These victories of the followers of Islam changed the history of the region in four important respects. First of all, Islam created a new commonwealth which paralleled what Cyrus had created in the name of tolerance and what Hammurabi constructed legally for the administration of justice among his people. Secondly, the coming of Islam into this part of the Middle East gave a *lingua franca* to peoples long babelised by waves of conquests and the continuous parading of nomadic lifestyles. Thirdly, the coming of Islam put an end to polytheism. Unlike the ancient rules who resorted to the politics of multiple deities for the sake of keeping the peace between the gods and goddesses on the one hand and their followers on the other, Islam brought all these varied peoples under one theological roof. Henceforth monotheism reinforces monogenesis, and human society was believed to be eternally linked by the chain of words from Heaven to this world. Last but not least, the coming of Islam made it categorically clear that rulers and the ruled are all accountable for their deeds on the day of judgment. This was a major transformation and both the Greek and the Persian were confronted with a new reality, the power of which was destined to haunt them for centuries.

The coming of Islam into modern day Iraq changed this part of the Middle East for good. Iraqis are very much aware of the fact that 637 A.D. was a turning point in their history, because less than five full years after the death of the Prophet of Islam, their society became a part of the emerging Muslim commonwealth. What makes this development significant is the fact that before the Islamic movement took over the Arabian Peninsula, pockets of Arabs existed in areas north of the Arabian Peninsula. These Arab settlements outside their original homelands were at Hira in the Euphrates, at Palmyra and at Nabataea in what is now called Jordan.

While we discuss the history of the region and how that history affects the course of events today, we should point out that the famous Battle of Qadisiyah in 637 A.D. which Saddam Hussein recalled with great malice towards the Iranians was actually a defeat of peoples living in his part of the Middle East by Arabic-speaking Muslims from the Arabian Peninsula. Qadisiyah can be described as an Arab victory only when you emphasize the Arabness of the fighters at the expense of their Islamic identity, an intellectual game that is definitely unacceptable to Muslims allergic to secular nationalisms. But, regardless of how one may feel about this political manipulation of world history, the fact still remains that Iraqis were conquered early by the Muslim armies and their destiny has since been deeply wedded to the Islamic movement. Evidences for this state of affairs can be found in the history of Iraq since the Muslim invasion. As Islam became more and more powerful, and as the contradictions within the Muslim *ummah* increasingly became evident, the peoples of Iraq found themselves willingly or unwittingly dancing to the tunes of great actors and forces in the region. The first major historical event involving the Iraqis was the succession question among the Companions of the Prophet. This became evident when Usman Ibn Affan, a first cousin and a chief Companion of the Prophet, was assassinated by dissidents who felt that his administration left much to be desired. The whole controversy surrounding this assassination and the manner in which the Muslims took sides later led to the polarization which pitted Iraq against Syria and the partisans of Ali (now called Shia) against the confederates of Muawiyah, a nephew of the assassinated Caliph and a powerful governor in Syria. Owing to this sectarian politics in early Islam, the Iraqis have come to be identified with the Shiite movement and the battles between Muawiyah and the descendants of Ali can undoubtedly be identified as the cause of friction between the Sunni majority in Islam and the Shiite minority.

The history of Islam in Iraq is not exclusively

confined to the saga and exploits of the Shiite shayks who fought the excesses of the Ummayyads ruling over the Islamic commonwealth. There were moments of reflections and meditations and as a result, a number of literary works have survived to the present times. Among modern Shiites, Kufah, Kerbala, and Najaf occupy pride of place among all the cities, towns, and villagers ever constructed by Shiites. The sense of reverence for these cities among the Shiites is primarily responsible for the present state of affairs in southern Iraq, where the government of Saddam Hussein found itself at loggerheads with elements of the Shiite community who strongly believe that the regime in Baghdad is not interested in the establishment of a religio-political order call Islamic governance (*Al-Wilayat al-Faqi*).

This concept of human governance based on the primacy of the *ahl-al-bait* (members of the Prophetic household) has become one of the key pillars of the Shiite doctrine of politics. Within the descendants of Ali two tendencies emerged. There was the Hassanian approach, which was based on compromise with Muawiyah. There also was the Husseinian approach, which was committed to the overthrow of what was then perceived as a corrupt Ummayyad dynasty. Unlike his brother who accepted money in exchange for the renunciation of his claims to his father's position as head of the Muslim *ummah*, Hussein challenged the regime of Muawiyah to the bitter end. When the former governor of the Syrian part of the Islamic commonwealth passed away, the mantle of leadership fell upon his son Yazid. It was this successor of Muawiyah who would face Ali's son, Hussein. Their bitter enmity and the resultant showdown led to the beheading of Hussein and the massacre of his party at Kerbala. Muslim historians narrate this tragic turn of events in Islamic history with great sorrow. But, like other human groupings, such developments in the history of Islam make it clear to Muslims and non-Muslims that the human condition is a mixed bag of moments of human callousness and moments when the milk of human kindness is shared with as many people as possible. Because of the gradual moral decay of the Ummayyad dynasty, the dissident groups, including the radical elements of the Shiites, found an effective propagandist in the person of Abu Muslim. It was on account of his efforts that the opposition to the Ummayyads materialized and a new dynasty called the Abbassids took over.

The collapse of the Ummayyad in 750 A.D. led to the transfer of the Muslim capital from Damascus in Syria to Baghdad in Iraq. This new center of gravity of the Muslim world would develop into a major civilization where philosophical, scientific, and literary works were produced in great numbers and Muslims became a major force in world history. During the Abbassid period Muslims were governed by some of the greatest administrative and political leaders in their history. However, as a result of the growing Persian influence the Muslim rulers of Baghdad increasingly became autocratic in their rule. Rather than maintain the tradition of the old Arab shaykh who was *primus inter pares* (first among equals), the caliphs at Baghdad soon established a new pattern of leadership which undermined the governance by *Shura* (consultation). Historians have identified seven Abbassid rulers as the ones whose rule contributed to the greater glory of this center of Islamic power in the Middle Ages. Ruling between 750 A.D. and 842 A.D. these men led the Muslims along the path of greater material opulence and cultural advancement. Of the seven, three are still celebrated in Muslim circles and beyond. Mansur (754-755) was the pioneer of this Muslim achievement in civilization-building. He transferred the Muslim capital from Damascus to Baghdad. Taking advantage of the water supplies of the area and the agreeable climatic condition, this Abbassid ruler soon transformed this site of ancient Ctesiphon into a very prosperous city. It is said that within thirty years, Baghdad became the second largest city in the Mediterranean.

Historians are unanimous on the fact that Harun Rashid was the greatest of all the Abbassid rulers because during his time the Muslims witnessed a renaissance. This renaissance brought power and glory to the Muslims of the Middle East and many neighboring peoples journeyed to the area in search of knowledge or opportunities. The achievements of Harun Rashid were added to by the progress in science, technology and material developments under the reign of his son Mamun. During the reign of Mamun Muslim poetry flourished and significant progress was made in the fields of historical studies, religious scholarship, and Arabic literature. The liberalism of Mamun created a tolerant atmosphere for diversity of views to exist within the Muslim *ummah*. This state of affairs did not last long, for after the demise of Mamun his successors reversed the trend towards liberalism and Islam came to be dominated by strictly orthodox forces.

Like the Ummayyad dynasty, the Abbassid too finally came to an end. However, unlike its predecessor, the Abbassid dynasty declined gradually. Inner decay and strife soon weakened the center and things began to fall away. The final day came when the Muslim armies in Baghdad were no longer strong enough to repel the advancing Mongols. As a result of this weakness the Mongols marched into the capital city of the Muslim world and destroyed it forever. Historians report that Baghdad was filled with blood of Muslims and the Tigris and Euphrates were darkened by the vast numbers of books thrown into them by these barbarians from central Asia.

Scholars writing on Islamic history have tried to identify the reasons for the collapse of this major Muslim center of civilization. One of the key factors identified with the decline is the conflict about the different schools of thought among the Muslims. As already pointed out, the coming to power of the Abbassid was the result of internal strife among the Muslims. The fact that the Abbassid were never fully accepted by the Shiites made their rule always tenuous and precarious. Determined to rule with or without Shiite support, and much aware of their growing material and political clout in the area, the Abbassid used force to keep the peace and to eliminate those who refused to come to terms with them. Added to this religious fragmentation was the increased sensitivity to ethnic origins. It should be remembered that, though the Persians were conquered by the Arab Muslim armies, they never felt it necessary to dissolve in the ocean of Arabism in order to be good Muslims. Determined to keep their ethnic and linguistic identity, these Persians would gradually enjoy greater power in Baghdad. Their greater visibility aroused ethnic jealousy and resentment. The problem of ethnic balance developed into a crisis when the Turks, who had earlier been recruited as slaves in the service of the ruling dynasty, became increasingly powerful. Charged with guarding and defending the caliphs, this body of foreign mercenaries and slaves soon became the kingmakers of the Muslim empire. This process was accelerated when Caliph Matasim transferred the capital to Samarra. Here the Turks had a field day as no rival power could check them and soon the caliphs were subject to the will and whims of the Turkish praetorian guards. This trend of events was eventually detrimental to the welfare of the Muslim empire, for soon many in the Muslim *ummah* began to resent the state of affairs at the center. The problem became more serious when the material splendor of the empire attracted the brightest and the best to the center. As a result of this areal and social mobility orthodoxy was gradually imposed from the center. However, as the leaders of the center tried to impose their interpretation of Islam on the rest of the *ummah*, those who had earlier challenged the legitimacy of the Abbassid found it unacceptable to be dictated to by the center. This ideological and doctrinal tug of war exposed the weaknesses of the center. But while we note the negative impact of this internal bickering on the future of the Abbassid dynasty, we should hasten to add that the Christian crusades also contributed to the changing fortunes of this Muslim empire. Many historians have noted this factor in the attempt at understanding the collapse of the Abbassid. For the purpose of this study which is looking at the past as it relates to the present Gulf crisis, one could state that the downfall of the Abbassid was the culmination of a series of political, social, and military setbacks which the rulers were not able to reverse.

The Mongol invasion of Iraq was the greatest disaster the people of this region had seen for centuries. The Iraqis have yet to recover from this tragedy. Hulagu, the grandson of Genghis Khan who carried out the conquest, could retrospectively be called the Adolf Hitler of the East, if one is allowed to use the analogy anachronistically. The Mongols defeated the Abbassid but failed to keep the conquered territories under their firm control. Soon dissension developed all over the empire and one dynasty succeeded the other. For a while it looked as if Tamerlane would restore Mongol hegemony, but this too failed. The fragmentation that came to be the reality of the time led to the parcelling out of old Abbassid territories into different spheres of influence. The old Arab tribes regrouped and began to press their claims which had been long suppressed and the Persians too staked their claims under the Safawid dynasty. This, however, was only for a brief period totalling less than thirty years. It was indeed this state of affairs that had existed among the Muslims of the Fertile Crescent that paved the way for the Ottomans. This rising power in Asia Minor had already eliminated the Seljuk Turks, a rival Turkish group that had exercised some hegemony in the region. As history would have it, this group of Turkish rulers would inherit the mantle of the Muslim caliphate after the capture of Egypt. This state of affairs came about as a result of the fact that, after the Mongol conquest of Baghdad, the Caliph fled to Cairo and continued to exercise some semblance of spiritual authority among the Muslims. With the conquest of Cairo by the Ottoman, their rulers combined the office of Sultan with that of Caliphate in 1517. The Ottoman were able to capture Baghdad in 1534 and for the first time since the Abbassid period, Muslims were able to have rulers who were both temporal and spiritual simultaneously. This state of affairs would continue within the Ottoman empire for several centuries. This pattern of governance would remain in force up until the seventeenth century when European powers began to challenge Muslim hegemony along the Mediterranean, the Red Sea area, and in the Indian Ocean. Portugal was the first European power to contest Muslim hegemony. Wrapping herself in the flag of Christianity and national interest, this southern European state began to inch her way along the African coastline toward the east. It should be remembered that at this time the Muslims controlled the gold, the spice, and the silk trade. Determined to have their share of this lucrative market and emboldened by the scientific and knowledge revolution of the time, the Portuguese soon staked their claims in Africa where the gold trade took place across the Sahara and in the Indian Ocean where the spice trade was monopolized by the Muslim traders.

The Portuguese threat to the Muslims in the east was resisted for some time. However, the entry into the fray by other western European powers soon led to greater conflicts between the Muslims and the European powers. This state of belligerency would become more serious as the curtain fell on the sixteenth century. By the seventeenth century the strategic significance of Iraq was quite evident to the competing Western powers. In order to gain a foothold in the region, these European powers began to challenge Muslim rulers in both Africa and Asia. Playing on the factionalism of the Arab groups of the Arabian Peninsula and North Africa, these Europeans soon began to challenge Muslim rulers in both Africa and Asia. This traditional divide-and-conquer strategy generally achieved its primary objective, as these Europeans soon began to gain ground at the expense of the Muslim states. With greater coordination among them, in spite of their own bickering and jockeying for power and territories, these rising European powers soon developed technologies which granted their supremacy in both Asia and Africa. Retrospectively, one could now argue that the Muslims became colonial subjects of European powers because they committed a number of strategic and political mistakes in which many of them were not clever enough to foresee their consequences. Owing to these circumstances, Muslims soon found themselves doing battle with Portuguese, Russians, Germans, French, Dutch, British, and Americans. The strategic significance of Iraq to the Russians rested in the fact that the Russians wanted access to the warm waters of the Mediterranean. The Black Sea and the Caucasus have provided access in the past. Befriending Iraq or bringing it under one political wing was desirable to the Russians. It was on account of this political calculation that the Russians worked out an entente with the British during the last century.

Yet, in tracing the history of the strategic significance of Iraq and its environs, one must take note of the fact that over the last century the contest for Iraq was largely between the Germans and the British. British strategists have argued that the Empire could only be maintained if and when the heartland of Asia and the sea lanes of the world were effectively under the control of the British navy. This strategic calculation had immediate implication for the Persian Gulf region. Too close to the Mediterranean and the Red Sea, and not too far from the Indian subcontinent, the Fertile Crescent became a key factor in the contest of will between the Germans and the Ottoman friends on the one hand and the British and their Russian allies on the other. This has come to be known to historians as the "great game."

The British rivalry with Germany affected the rulers of the Gulf in that each European power decided to exploit Arab and Muslim differences. On the Arabian Peninsula, two leading families were locked in a mortal war of all against all. The Rashid family of Hail and the Saud family in Nejd became the fighters to be used as proxies in the grand European game. The Rashids were both pro-Turkish and pro-German. The Saudis, on the other hand, were anti-Turkish and had greater sympathies for the British. The Germans were also interested in Kuwait because they wanted to use it as the terminal point for their Berlin-to-Baghdad rail project. This dream was never to be realized because the British made sure that the Amir of Kuwait, Shaykh Mubarak, was not in favor of the idea. This great game of the European powers continued up to the outbreak of the First World War.

In looking for the historical background to the present Gulf crisis, one is forced to re-examine the circumstances and conditions leading to the eruption of the First World War. From our vantage point, we can argue that the German-Turkish alliance was seen as a threat to British interest in the Gulf and this was demonstrated quite effectively by the British when they dispatched a force to Iraq soon after hostilities broke out. The Iraqis found themselves as pawns in this deadly game of the superpowers when the German-Turkish command decided to resist any British intrusion into the area. To safeguard their interest further, the British worked out open and secret deals with Arab rulers in the area. One of the most significant deals struck by the British was that which brought Sherif Hussein of Mecca into the conflict. Convinced that he and his progeny would be elevated as rulers of the Arabs, and determined to check the hegemony of the Turks in the region, Sherif Hussein and his children threw their lot with the British and thus antagonized the Turks and their supporters elsewhere in the Muslim world. This alliance between the Hashemites and the British became a reality in 1915, when Hussein received guarantees from Sir Henry McMahon, High Commissioner for Egypt, that the Arabs would obtain political independence in exchange for support for the British war effort. Under the terms of this secret agreement, one understands that the British were not willing to hand over control of all Arab lands. The conditional clause specifically addresses the need to guarantee the security of non-Arabic speaking minorities. Added to this conditionality was another which stipulates that special administrative guarantees be made to safeguard mutual economic interests.

The present day system in Iraq is actually the result of the deadly game of the superpowers in the late nineteenth century and early twentieth century. Following the defeat of the central powers in the First World War, the Arabs who had earlier rallied to the Allied Powers rushed to press their claims. In anticipation of the end of the war, Amir Faisal, the son of Sherif Hussein of Mecca, journeyed to Paris where the peace treaty among the European powers was being hammered out. He thought, perhaps naively, that the British and French were going to fulfill promises made to him directly or through his son, Faisal. The Hashemites did not reap any immediate benefits from the Paris peace talks. Rather, the British and their French counterparts succeeded in placing these Muslim lands under mandatory regimes. Iraq soon became one of these territories. Taking note of these changing times, Amir Faisal went to Paris to attend as observer and petitioner on behalf of the Arabs. After having shed blood in the name of anti-Turkish rule in Arab world, this Arab leader and his supporters sought the cooperation of the Allied Powers to safeguard their territories. This was not to be. Even when the Arab nationalists of Syria voted Faisal as the king of Syria and Transjordan, the French refused to comply. The Allied

Powers however, agreed at San Remo to put Iraq and Palestine under the British government.

This new imperial order was soon caught in the web of controversy and nationalist agitation. Unwilling to accept the colonial idea of subjecting Arab lands to outsiders, and determined to be free at all costs, the Iraqi people embarked on a national struggle for liberation. By 1920, the battle lines were beginning to be drawn. Historians have identified a number of factors which they believe were responsible. Some have argued that Arab notions of freedom and tribal tendencies toward schism were partly to be blamed for Arab political disunity at the time. Others have suggested that the question of taxation and the traditional suspicion of government were important factors in the final showdown between the colonial, mandated authority and the nationalists of Iraq. When the fight broke out between the warring forces, the British at first had difficulty in bringing the situation under control. Ultimately the authorities were able to bring an end to this menace. The British, as history would have it, later accepted the revolt as a lesson in imperial fence-building. At the end of this struggle, the British worked out a *modus vivendi* with the nationalists. The outcome of that negotiation guaranteed British investments and put an end to the occupation.

As a result of the compromise in the aftermath of the Iraqi revolt, a new administration was allowed to operate. The British learned their lessons from this major upheaval known as the Iraqi National War of Liberation. As soon as the dust settled, the British opened lines of communications with emerging leaders of the Iraqi people. They oversaw the election of Amir Faisal as the king of the Iraqis on August 23, 1921. This new leadership for the Iraqis and the new attitude of the

British combined to create a new situation for the constitutional experiment in Iraq. Within a ten year period the British worked out the necessary arrangements for independence with the Iraqi leaders around them. They signed a treaty which replaced the Mandate. They also sponsored the new state of Iraq for membership in the League of Nations. In order to protect their interests and to not be caught in the crossfire of inter-Arab politics, they arranged a treaty of friendship between Iraq and Saudi Arabia in 1936. The fortunes of Iraq rose rapidly in these early days because of the oil resources she possessed. It is estimated that as early as 1932 one quarter of the entire national revenue was derived from oil. This national resource helped solve a number of the social and political problems faced by the newly independent country.

When we look at the legacies of British rule in Iraq, we find that the British contributed directly or indirectly to the hegemony of the Sunni minority in Iraq. It was British officers who created the conditions for this state of affairs to develop in the country. Related to this is the predominance of the landed groups of aristocrats who continued to exercise influence even after the overthrow of the monarchy in 1958. Another legacy of British rule in Iraq was the polarization of the Iraqis along linguistic, religious, and regional lines. These were fissures which the British exploited skillfully to their advantages. But regardless of one's opinions about British rule and legacies, the fact remains that the British were as effective as the Iraqi leaders and people let them be. Principal among the forces responsible for British influence in Iraq was King Faisal. This was evident after his death in 1933.

Many historians have traced the rise in military intervention in Iraqi politics to the early years after the death of King Faisal, including the military suppression of the Assyrian revolt, and the suppression of the Euphrates tribes. Explanations for this military intervention include the fact that there were no national leaders comparable to the late King Faisal. People like Nuri as-Said were not yet widely known. During this transitional period military men were impressed by the military distinction. Between 1936 and 1941 seven military coup d'etats took place. Of these revolts the most serious was that of 1941. The violent encounter between the Iraqi forces and the British took place because Rashid Ali al-Gilani, the leader of the revolt, took power and set up a new government which was hostile to British interest. In order to dislodge him from power, the British sought and got the military cooperation of the Arab Legion of Transjordan. Following the suppression of the Gilani revolt, the succeeding governments cooperated fully with the British. But this was not to last for long because other more powerful forces were in the making and soon the British hegemony would be challenged by the forces of pan-Arabism of both the Nasserite variety and of the Baathist variety.

During this period the spirit of pan-Arabism began to spread among them. Soon the incoherence of the ideology began to receive attention and within a matter of a decade or less, new forces committed to the unity of all the Arab peoples began to assert themselves. To counter these negative forces and to consolidate the powers of the monarchies of the region loyal to them, the British and the wartime American allies began to devise ways of building a grand alliance that would form a *cordon sanitaire* around the communist world. Known to history as the Baghdad Pact, this treaty provided the framework within which the pro-Western governments of alliance in the Middle East did not go down well with the Arab states listening to Nasser. Committed to the principles of pan-Arabism, and dead serious about the unification of the Arab peoples, Nasser preached vehemently against the Baghdad Pact. This anti-imperialism of Nasser would soon endear him to millions of Arabs and his radio messages would inspire thousands from around the Arab world.

Another British legacy that would affect Iraqi society and history is the decision to create a homeland for the Jews in Palestine. This decision of the British government was destined to lead to bloody wars between Arabs and Jews up to the present time. Conscious of their history, and fully aware of what other Arabs and Muslims would say if they stayed away from the struggle against the Hebrew state, the Iraqis entered the conflict when war broke out between the two groups. Since their first involvement in the first Arab-Israeli War, the Iraqis have produced charismatic leaders who have continued to assert Iraqi identity within Arab/Muslim circles. And their success in this venture has largely benefitted from the oil revenues. With the discovery and marketing of oil, Iraq was now destined to be one of the key players in the region.

This significance of Iraq was the result of the combination of three factors. The first was its continuing strategic relevance; the second relates to the large deposits of oil found by the British in the country; and the third was the historical place and role of this valuable piece of real estate resting between the Tigris and the Euphrates. These three factors were not missed by both General Kassem and President Saddam Hussein. General Kassem, who successfully executed the first coup d'etat in 1958, was a radical with leftist notions about life, society and history. However, before this new Iraqi ruler felt comfortable in his place, a coup d'etat took place and his life was brought to an end. Between his time and the present the Iraqis witnessed the rise of several military men. Of these the only one who has been able to last for long is President Saddam Hussein. Why has he been successful in keeping himself in power? He has been able to do so because he established a tyranny that instills fear among his opponents and fear in the hearts of his friends and supporters who might be swayed by treacherous friends against him. Transformed into the Republic of Fear, and reduced to a society where the pre-eminence of a person is measured in terms of one's loyalty to the Baath philosophy in general and Saddam himself in particular, Iraq soon became a hell to many Iraqis.

Since he came to power in the 1970s, he has managed to create the state in his own image. This is to say, he has succeeded in making the people afraid of him. And to add insult to injury he has proclaimed himself the great leader and compatriot of the Arab and Muslim peoples. This chapter cannot exhaust the subject here. However, it should be noted that the eruption of the Iran-Iraq War was destined to create many problems for the Arab and Muslim world. Not only did it divide the Arab states, but it also created an atmosphere of tension within the international system. This climate of negative opinion of the West has generated a great deal of uneasiness and uncertainty.

It is indeed against this historical background that one discusses the Iraqi invasion of Kuwait. The invasion of a neighboring Muslim country sent the wrong signal. It exposed five great weaknesses within the Iraqi society. The first and most serious weakness was the total absence of democratic governance and the Islam-based principle of consultation (Shura). The second was the militarization of Iraqi society and the negative consequences of regimentation. The third weakness is the inability of the Iraqi people to reverse the process of tyrannical rule through their greater visibility and agitation. The fourth weakness is in the maintenance of a political order based on the hegemony of a Sunni minority. Last but not least, the Iraqi society has not been able to determine its future because the excesses of both the dictator and the excess of the foreign interlopers makes it very difficult. It is owning to this delicate interplay between domestic calculations for political survival and external inducements for military action that Iraq now suffers the wrath of the world.

In the rest of this book we examine the Gulf crisis, taking into account the various facets of the story of the Gulf War. Each of the chapters in the book is designed in such a way that the events of 1990-91 come alive once again. The only significant difference this time is that the reader is not looking at main frames portraying faraway events whose historical roots and contemporary significance are not clearly spelled out. The story of the Gulf crisis is told from the perspective of the Saudi policymakers. Though we have not been able to interview each and every key player in the war against "the father of all invaders," we have the confidence that what we have collected within these pages gives us sufficient food for thought. Hopefully, those who take the time to go over the entire book will walk away with some insights and probably a new perspective not only on Iraqi blunders in Kuwait but on the very nature of the Middle East political situation and the different variables that conspire to keep it in the news. But, regardless of your political leanings and ideological proclivities, the fact still remains that the Kuwaitis and other Gulf people, including the Saudis, now know that there is indeed a life after Saddam's brutal invasion. Some would retort to this statement by asking: At what price? It is to this and other related questions we now turn for greater analysis and discussion.

---

1. Harris, George L. *Iraq. Its People, Its Society, Its Culture*, 1958, pg. 7.
2. Ibid. pg. 8.

2

THE SADDAM FACTOR: RISE OF AN IRAQI "PRINCE"

It is perhaps fitting that one of Saddam Hussein's first acts of national significance came October 7, 1959, when as a 23-year-old officer he and scores of Baath party military officers unsuccessfully attempted to assassinate Iraqi President Abdul al-Karim Qasim. Saddam was able to escape the police and ultimately fled to Egypt, where he lived in exile until 1963, when the Baathists' military coup succeeded in finally overthrowing Qasim. In the summer of 1961, Qasim tried to annex Kuwait, but the effort was reversed when it met with sudden and unified opposition from members of the Arab League.[1] Qasim's ill-advised incursion into Kuwait caused many to question his judgment, as it soured relations with his neighbors for many years. But it is said that Saddam Hussein, while in Egypt, sent a message to Qasim, whom he had tried to assassinate only two years earlier, congratulating him on his "brilliant" move.

When the Baathists overthrew Qasim in 1963, it began a brutal campaign against one of his principle supporters, the Iraqi Communist Party. After expanding the National Guard from 5,000 to 34,000, the Baathists rounded up ICP members in their homes, often executing or torturing leaders. Although reliable numbers of deaths were never available, it was clear that thousands were arrested and sports grounds were turned into makeshift prisons to hold the flow of detainees.[2]

King Hussein of Jordan has been quoted as saying that the February 1963 slaughter of ICP members "had the support of American intelligence," which was concerned that the ICP was emerging as the strongest communist party in the Middle East.[3]

Indeed, the violence appeared to be carried out methodically, as if newly empowered Baath officials were armed with lists of enemies provided by the Central Intelligence Agency. A former State Department official confirmed to two authors that in the late 1950s and early 1960s, Saddam Hussein and other Baathists had made contact with American authorities, stating that the Baaths were the political force of the future and deserving of American support against Qasim and the Communists."[4]

A central story of modern Iraq is the emergence of the Baath Party as the main power, and Saddam Hussein's rise to prominence within the party machine. The Baath Party in fact was founded in Damascus in 1944 by three French-educated Syrian intellectuals, Michel Alfaq (a Greek Orthodox Christian), Salah al-Din Bitar (a Sunni Muslim), and Zaki al-Arsuzi (an Alawite).[5] Inception of the party was seen as a response to France's colonial hold over Syria. Given European control over the Middle East, it was not surprising that Baathism became an attractive philosophy for Arab nationalists. The philosophical underpinnings of Iraqi Baathism were somewhat vague, as it embraced socialist concepts of land reform, free social education, and medical services, but rejected communist notions of class conflict and struggle. The general Baath view was that liberation from western control would lead to development and modernization which, in turn, would solve most social problems.

However, Iraqi Baaths were not overly interested in ideology or debates. In the 1960s, most electoral activity was restricted to executive committees of labor and professional unions and was usually dominated by the communists. Instead, the Iraqi Baaths relied upon their keen ability to organize geographically based para-military groups capable of inflicting terror on their opponents, the most notorious of which were associated with Saddam Hussein and Sabah Mirza in Juayfir and Karkh, or Ali Salih al-Saadi in Bab al-Shaikh.[6]

In the years following the 1963 overthrow of Qassim, rival Baath groups, along with Nasserists and Communists, jockeyed for power in what turned out to be a fluid government. One Baath "gang" leader, Ali Salih al-Saadi, embarked on such an extraordinary campaign of murder and terror against opponents immediately following the coup, that he was forced out as Minister of the Interior.[7]

Between 1963 and 1968, the Iraqi leadership changed three times, with even more tumult at the ranks below. It is worth noting that in the autumn of 1965, while President Abdullah al-Salam Arif and his foreign minister were at a meeting in Casablanca, Morocco, Air Force Commander Arif Abdullah al-Razzaq unsuccess-fully tried a coup and had to flee the country. President Arif had named al-Razzaq air force commander only eight weeks before, indicating that loyalty of political appointees was not guaranteed.

In July 1968, there was a two-stage coup carried out by opponents of Arif. In the first stage, Abdullah al-Rahman al-Daaud, commander of the Republican Guard took over the radio station, while others took charge of the Ministry of Defense. Al-Daaud, was named new Defense Minister. While al-Daaud was visiting Jordan for a troop inspection, Saddam Hussein, acting on orders of the new President Ahmad Hasan al-Bakr, arrested al-Daaud's allies, including the new Prime Minister Abdullah al-Razzaq al-Nayif, who previously had served as director of military intelligence.

The 1968 coup established the al-Bakr-Saddam Hussein wing of the Baath Party as the rulers of Iraq. In the ensuing years, Saddam Hussein devoted his energy to consolidating powers by either dismissing his opponents or more gradually easing them out of power. In 1973, a poorly planned coup against al-Bakr, during one of his rare visits out of the country, was foiled. The plotter, Nadhim Kazzar, was appointed by Saddam Hussein to head the security services in 1969, and had gained the reputation as a sadistic torturer and murderer, and eliminated many enemies of the Baath party over a four-year span.[8] Consequently, al-Bakr and Hussein continued to tighten their grip on power, reducing the ruling Revolutionary Command Council (RCC) to seven members.

Throughout the 1970s, Saddam Hussein continued to expand his power within the Revolutionary Command Council. Moreover, it was after the 1973 Arab-Israeli War that Iraq and Saudi Arabia, finding themselves between a de facto Israeli-Iranian alliance, began to repair their chilly relations, a process which ultimately resulted in huge windfalls for Saddam Hussein, and helped him survive his mistaken invasion of Iran.

In June 1975, for instance, then Crown Prince Fahd paid a visit to Baghdad, resulting in an agreement of the delimitation of the neutral zone on the borders between the two countries. In the course of his speech on the seventh anniversary of the Baath Party's seizure of power on July 17, 1975, President al-Bakr declared that "in accordance with our clear pan-Arab outlook we have sought to deepen understanding with the Arab countries of the Gulf, particularly Saudi Arabia, and to solve the issues pending with them."[9]

It was during this period that Iraq came to an agreement with Kuwait on its long-standing border dispute.[10]

The main target of Iraq's reconciliation campaign was Saudi Arabia, which maintained a clear financial and moral commitment to Syria, Iraq's chief rival at the time. In April 1976, in the course of a visit to Jeddah, Saddam Hussein affirmed the need for joint action between Saudi Arabia "and all the states of the Gulf," and in October 1977 a series of important joint technical and trade agreements was announced.[11]

This was accompanied by the first large financial aid packages to Iraq from Saudi Arabia and the Gulf states.[12] This period of renewed relations and Saudi aid culminated in February 1979, in the immediate aftermath of the Iranian revolution, when Saudi Arabia and Iraq signed a security treaty. Subsequently, in April 1979, Saddam Hussein, seeking to demonstrate his anti-Communist credentials, declared that Iraq would never allow Saudi Arabia to be occupied by the Soviet Union.[13]

As mentioned, the improvement in Saudi Arabia's relations with Iraq was driven by the desire to shore up regional alliances in the face of a hostile and expansive Israel to the West. By 1979, an even more urgent threat was present from the Ayatollah Khomeini-led Iranian revolution, which vowed to export its brand of Islamic radicalism to its closest neighbors. Given these circumstances, basic geopolitical concerns would have propelled Saudi Arabia and Iraq to improve relations whomever the leadership at the time.

It was significant, however, that this period of fence-mending paralleled the time-frame when Saddam Hussein successfully consolidated his power within the RCC, and ultimately became the country's undisputed leader.

Up until 1976 there were several individuals vying for leadership of the RCC. But by January 1976, after a series of power plays, the two remaining candidates were Saddam Hussein and al-Bakr. It was that month that Saddam, who had no military background, was "promoted" to the rank of general, retrospectively from July 1, 1973. A few weeks later, it was announced that the complement of the People's Militia, the Baath Party's own military force under the command of Taha Yasin Ramadan would be doubled; over the next few years, its equipment was gradually built up sufficiently for it to be able to act, if necessary, as a counterweight to the regular armed forces. In October 1977, al-Bakr handed over the portfolio of defense to his son-in-law, Colonel Adnan Khairallah, who also was the brother of Saddam's wife. In April 1978, Khairallah, then 38, was promoted to the rank of general. In addition, the various internal security services grouped together under the General Directorate of Intelligence reported directly to Saddam, generally through his cousin Sadun Shakir, and surveillance and control of the Baath Party organization were institutionalized through "morale officers" and Party commissars, who also reported directly to Vice President Saddam Hussein.

By September 1977, Saddam Hussein and his small group of allies succeeded in absorbing the Baath Regional Command into the RCC, which signified the end of the Baath Party as an independent body. One of the first "decisions" of the enlarged RCC was to issue a decree transferring all aspects of oil policy and oil marketing from the Ministry of Oil to the "Follow-Up Committee for Oil Affairs and Implementation of Agreements, now to be chaired by Vice President and RCC deputy Chairman Saddam Hussein." The decree stipulated that Hussein, in effect, was "responsible for all aspects of oil policy, coordination and operations, and that no decision on oil marketing could be taken without his approval."[14]

With power increasingly consolidated, the Baath-run Iraqi government once again turned to its internal threats, which it always linked to various external threats. It stepped up its clamp down on Shiite Muslim demonstrators; it began a brutal anti-communist campaign in the spring of 1978; it embarked upon a ruthless scorched earth policy against the Kurdish population and several executions and dismissals took place within the armed forces. At the same time, Saddam Hussein tried out as a foreign policy statesman by taking charge of the Baghdad Summit and exploring reconciliation with Syria.

By the summer of 1979, the table was set for Saddam's official assumption of power. On July 16, 1979, the eve of the eleventh anniversary of the Baath takeover, al-Bakr appeared on television to announce his resignation, and Saddam Hussein was "sworn in" immediately as president. In his speech, al-Bakr commended Hussein as the best man for the post and enthusiastically endorsed him. Izzat al-Duri, a loyal lieutenant of Saddam, was appointed vice president. A few days before al-Bakr's resignation, Muhi Abd al-Hussein Mashhadi was replaced by Tariq Hamad al-Abdullah.

Saddam's power grab climaxed 12 days later, on July

28, 1979, when it was declared that a plot to overthrow the regime, masterminded by the Syrians, had been uncovered. A special court of seven RCC members was formed, and within a few days, twenty-two people, including Mashadia and four of his colleagues on the RCC, were executed. These "democratic executions" were carried out in person by Saddam Hussein and the remaining members of the leadership; the trials and confessions of the guilty parties were filmed and circulated as proof of the plotters' guilt.

As the Slugletts wrote in their excellent book, *Iraq Since 1958: From Revolution to Dictatorship.*"This episode was particularly remarkable in view of the fact that many of those executed had been among Saddam Hussein's most intimate associates, particularly (Adnan) Hamdani, a close personal friend of long standing. The fact that even those close to him could fall so suddenly and fatally from favor was clear for all to see, and it was evident that no opposition whatsoever, whether inside or outside the Party, would be tolerated. . . .While the extent of Syrian involvement will never be known, Saddam made full use of the allegation as a means of ridding the regime of any pressing obligations to consummate the much-vaunted union between the two countries."[15]

In 1975, when Iraq began repairing its relations with its Arab Gulf neighbors, it also moved to improve its relations with Iran while the Shah was still firmly in charge. This led to marathon negotiations in March 1975 between Saddam Hussein, while he was deputy commander of the RCC, and the Shah, which produced a communique that became the basis for the Algerian Treaty. The communique and subsequent treaty allowed for divided use of the Shatt-al-Arab waterway, settled other border disputes and stopped both nations from supporting each other's Kurdish struggles for independence.

Iranian journalist Behrouz Sourerafil wrote, "The period from 1975 to 1979 was the only period of peaceful co-existence between the two countries and was the only period in which although all disputes between the two countries were not resolved, the Iranian and Iraqi governments had friendly relations with each other."[16]

Ayatollah Khomeini had spent several years agitating against the Shah from Iraqi soil. But in October 1978, Saddam Hussein ordered Khomeini to leave, stating, "We accepted Ayatollah Khomeini in our country at a time when he was sentenced to death, but since he was continuing his political activities, he had to leave Iraq. . . We respect religious leaders but we do not expect them to replace political leaders."[17]

The revengeful Khomeini, who was said to hate Saddam for his non-religious political ideas, never forgave Saddam for his expulsion to Paris. When Khomeini assumed power in February 1979, he immediately initiated a war of words with the Iraqi leader.

Much of the writing about the roots of the dispute between Iran and Iraq has focused on the Shatt-al-Arab waterway, sometimes referred to as the "barometer" of relations between the two countries. However, the true importance of the waterway must be lessened when one considers that it was divided for both nations' use by the Algerian Treaty, and is wide enough to accommodate both of their needs.

A more important factor was the personality and world view of Saddam and Khomeini. In hindsight, it seems only natural that when two megalomaniacal personalities are positioned at the head of two oil rich countries and two large and powerful armies, they will become extremely dangerous neighbors.

By December 1979, Khomeini implied to European reporters that Saddam's days were numbered, stating, "It is possible that some Muslim heads of state end up with a destiny like the Shah's."[18] The same day Iranian demonstrators shouted slogans against Iraq, comparing Saddam with President Jimmy Carter and Israeli Prime Minister Menachem Begin.

There were many border skirmishes between Iraqi and Iranian armies along the border from January 1980 to when war broke out, September 22, 1980. Subsequently, Mohammad Mashat, the Iraqi ambassador to France, said Iran committed 548 invasions of various kinds against Iraq and Baghdad delivered 147 protests to Tehran. On the other hand, Iranians had registered 637 acts of Iraqi aggression, prompting 53 protests from Tehran.[19]

While Saddam certainly did not appreciate either Khomeini's comments or the demonstrations, what may have really caught his attention was Khomeini's invitation to Iraqi Kurdish leaders to visit Iran and plan a resumption of their struggle against Iraq.

Saddam probably felt Khomeini's obsession with exporting his Iranian-style Islamic revolution, and inciting the Iraqi Shiite population against Baghdad, was enough of a threat to consider action against Iran. But the prospect of the return of the Kurdish rebellion, with which Saddam had bitter, personal experiences in suppressing in the past, may have been too much to fathom.

On the "positive" side, Saddam most likely saw a divided Iran ready to be plucked like ripe fruit, as the military leadership, built up over the years by the Shah, was seriously weakened by executions and imprisonment.

A weakened Iran might also be more prepared to cooperate with Iraq on the Kurds, as the Shah had done.

The grander vision might have been determinant, though, considering Saddam's goal of becoming the "Nasser," or undisputed leader of the region. A quick victory over Iran would have brought Saddam a giant step closer to his dream of being "master" of the Gulf, and thus would have catapulted him into the position of one of the most important leaders in the Arab world. On the geopolitical level, he undoubtedly knew that the United States' dissatisfaction with Iran over the hostage issue would bring America to his side. Moreover, the Gulf Cooperation Council nations' fear of Iranian-style Islamic radicalism would force them into his corner as well. As the Sluglett's put it, "Given his high self-esteem and his belief in the insurmountable economic might of his country, the temptation to launch the war seems to have become irresistible."[20]

Anyone objectively analyzing the region could quickly see how badly Saddam and his RCC clique had miscalculated when choosing to launch their September 22, 1980, invasion of Iran.

While it was true the Iranian military was in unprecedented disarray, Saddam and company either overlooked or discounted the fact that Iran's population of 42 million was roughly three times that of Iraq's 13.5 million. Second, Tehran, the seat of power, was about 850 kilometers from Baghdad, 650 of which are inside Iran. Not even the superiority of Iraq's impressive armored divisions could overcome those distances. Third, Iraq was potentially vulnerable to counterattacks, due to the two countries' common border of 1,300 kilometers.

Beyond these vital numbers, there were grave miscalculations about the peoples of Iran and Iraq.

Possibly due to his paranoia, as well as his desire to maintain absolute and total control over his population, Saddam Hussein overestimated the degree to which the Iraqi Shiite population as a whole was in sympathy with, or prepared to support the establishment of a theocratic regime in Iraq.

More importantly from a strategic point of view, he badly underestimated the extent to which the Iranian masses were inspired by Khomeini's anti-Shah, anti-imperialist brand of fundamentalism, and were prepared to enlist in the all-out jihad against Saddam, the newest, local version of the "Great Satan."

In a sense, these miscalculations were a product of the law of cause and effect. Saddam Hussein had succeeded so dramatically in narrowing the ruling circle that it became an isolated clique of "yes men" dedicated to the personality cult of its leader. Although their deliberations were quite secret, it is plain to see that no RCC members seriously challenged Saddam's views in any major way. If Saddam thought that Iran was weakened by the Khomeini revolution and could be brought to its knees by a swift strike by the Iraqi army, no member of the RCC would convince him otherwise. Most likely, RCC members came up with reasons to support Saddam's thinking.

Not only was Saddam not confronted with opposing views within his ruling circle that could have helped him see the world more objectively, however he had an astounding lack of first-hand familiarity with his own neighbors, as he was, quite possibly, the world's least-travelled head of state. This too was no accident. It is important to note that most of the coups of Iraqi heads of state and removals of various ministers during Saddam's rise to power occurred when those about to lose their power had travelled outside of Iraq. Although it was sometimes said in jest by outsiders that Saddam never wanted to leave Iraq for fear of a coup, Saddam most certainly understood that there was a distinct historical basis for such fear, particularly considering that he himself helped designed plots to remove his predecessors based upon their travel plans.

The element of surprise and the disarray of Iranian forces enabled Iraq to achieve some early victories. But within a year, Iran had rallied and began putting Iraq on the defensive. The turn of events sent shudders through the Gulf countries, as well as the West, as they contemplated the implications of Iran overrunning its neighbors and exporting its revolution through its presence much the same way the Red Army founded "communism" in Eastern Europe.

The subsequent aid contributed to Iraq was a key factor in preventing an Iranian takeover and preserving Saddam's hold on power. When Iran appeared to take the offensive in the fall of 1982, the Gulf states began providing Iraq with $1 billion a month in various forms of aid. Although the rate levelled off quickly, the aid totals steadily mounted. Kuwait reportedly provided $17 billion over eight years in currency and oil alone. This figure did not include loans from western banks that Kuwait had guaranteed on behalf of Iraq, the total of which may have been as high as $10 billion. The Kuwaitis also became Iraq's port, as the war had put the Basra facility out of commission.

Saudi Arabia later calculated its contributions at $25 billion over eight years. This came in the form of $5.85 billion in "non-repayable aid"; $9.24 billion in "soft cash loans"; $95 million in development loans; $3.74 billion in military equipment and logistics; $6.75 billion in petroleum aid; $16.7 million in-kind value of industrial products for reconstruction of Basra; $20.26 million for

"SABIC;" and $21.3 million for 270 construction vehicles.[21]

The United States provided key support, ranging from intelligence that enabled the Iraq military to target Iranian assets to agricultural imports and other aid.

Of course, the countries supporting Iraq were concerned with the threat posed by the Khomeini regime and his quest for Islamic fanaticism. But the price they paid for the short-sighted goal of using Iraq to stop Iran was the strengthening and empowerment of Saddam Hussein at a time when he should have been most vulnerable.

For American, European, and Israeli arms dealers who reaped enormous profits, the conflict was a dream come true. For Israel there was the added benefit of seeing the Iraqi army, the one it feared the most, thoroughly occupied and facing the other direction for eight years, as it expanded illegal settlements in the occupied West Bank and continued regular military raids into Lebanon at will.

The Iran-Iraq War was a disaster for both countries. Total casualties were estimated at 1,000,000. Soldiers and even children died in battles reminiscent of the horrible trench warfare of World War I. The Iraqis brought back another feature from that era: chemical warfare.

With the death toll reaching horrendous proportions, the economies of the two countries collapsing, and the futility of the war so obvious and expensive that not even Saddam and Khomeini could afford to ignore it, all rhetoric was put aside and a cease fire was signed.

Tried as he might, there was little about which Saddam Hussein could credibly claim victory. He gained no territory. Hundreds of thousands of his people died.

The direct cost of the war to Iraq was estimated at $175 billion, with major portions of that going for arms purchases.[22] Iraq had wiped out its foreign reserves. As early as August 1983, Iraq's foreign reserves had fallen to $3 billion from $30 billion three years earlier.[23] By 1985, its foreign debt had skyrocketed to $40 billion.

By the end of the war, Iraq's foreign debt was estimated at $60 billion. Saddam knew there would be minimal pressure on repayment of most of this sum. About $30 billion was owed to Saudi Arabia, Kuwait, and other Gulf countries which could be counted on to be patient. Another $20 billion was owed to the Soviet Union or Eastern Europe countries. However, some $10 billion was owed to western, mainly U.S. banks. While Kuwait had guaranteed some of these loans, Saddam eventually would have to find a way to handle repayment or face severe problems in the world of international finance which, in turn, could frustrate any future moves toward rebuilding his country or other economic programs.[24]

On the other hand, things could have been much worse. While Basra was decimated by various battles, most of Iraq, including Baghdad, was not damaged by the war. Iraq's oil and chemical installations were largely in tact. With the exception of Syria, Iraq had improved its ties to its neighboring Gulf countries and the West. Most important to Saddam, he was still very much in control.

---

1. Dann, Uriel. *Iraq Under Qassem: A Political History,* London, 1969, pgs. 349-53.
2. Sluglett. op cit. pg. 86.
3. Batatu, Hanna. *The Old Social Classes and the Revolutionary Movements of Iraq: A Study of Iraq's Old Landed and Commercial Classes and of*

Its Communists, Baathists and Free Officers,
Princeton, 1978, pgs. 1011-12.

4. Sluglett. pg. 283.
5. Sluglett. pg. 87.
6. Sluglett. pgs. 92-93.
7. Sluglett. pg. 92.
8. Rouleau, Eric. *Le Monde,* July 19 & 21, 1973.
9. British Broadcasting Company short-wave
   Broadcasts, June 7, 1975 & July 19, 1975, as
   cited in Marion Farouk-Sluglett and Peter Sluglett.
   Iraq Since 1958: from Revolution to Dictatorship,
   KPI Limited, London, 1987.
10. BBC, SWB. June 26, 1975, as cited by Sluglett.
11. ARR. October 3, 1977. as cited by Sluglett.
12. ARR. April 17, August 12 & October 3, 1977.
13. *Guardian*, April 11, 1979.
14. *Middle East Economic Survey,* Sept. 19, 1977.
15. Ibid., pg. 209.
16. Sourerafil, Behrouz. *The Iran-Iraq War,* Guinan
    Lith. Co. [New York], 1989.
17. Ibid., pg. 23.
18. *Ettela'at Newspaper* - Tehran Edition, December
    1, 1979.
19. Balta, Paul. *Iran-Iraq: Ine Guerre de 500 Ans.,*
    Paris: Anthropos, 1987, pgs. 130-131.
20. Sluglett. pg. 257.
21. Message from King Fahd to PresidentSaddam
    Hussein, Jan. 16, 1991, as reprinted in *Arab
    News,* January 17, 1991.
22. *The Iran-Iraq War,* pg. 132.
23. Sluglett. pg. 265.
24. *The Iran-Iraq War,* pg. 135.

3

IRAQ, KUWAIT AND THE ROAD TO WAR

The end of the Iran-Iraq War in August 1988 prompted various political and business leaders around the world to visit Baghdad.

Many were interested in the post-war economic opportunities, knowing that the Basra area was in need of total reconstruction, and that the country in general would be a renewed and willing market for many products.

But the constraints on Iraq caused by the large foreign debt and low cash reserves dampened some of the initial enthusiasm for doing business there. This in turn must have produced new frustrations for Saddam Hussein, who most likely was counting on foreign investment and a construction boom to help him sidestep the post-war recession that more typically occurs when large numbers of people are transferred from military service to the civilian economy.

A main part of Iraq's post-war strategy was an increase in oil revenues through the expansion of production. Consequently, when oil prices began to drop in 1989, it was more than an unpleasant surprise, it constituted a major drop in the nation's main source of income, and meant that Saddam had miscalculated again. His initial plan for Iraq's post-war recovery was not going according to script.

There were indications that Saddam Hussein, in seeking a way out of his growing economic problems, was at least contemplating, if not beginning to plan, some sort of move against his oil-rich neighbor in Kuwait.

In late 1988 King Fahd accepted Saddam's invitation to visit Baghdad as part of a celebration of the end of the Iran-Iraq War. During the visit, Saddam surprised King Fahd with an Iraqi-Saudi "non-aggression pact," an unusual move in the world of international diplomacy where most agreements are negotiated and drawn up prior to the leaders' meeting. It was also unusual in the sense that in the previous eight years, Saudi Arabia had contributed $25 billion in aid to Iraq, to help it defend itself against the Iranian offensive and rebuild its infrastructure. But King Fahd, ever the polite guest, did not want to offend his host and signed the accord. A similar pact was struck between Iraq and Bahrain.

When viewed in its historical context, Saddam's surprise non-aggression pact carried strong signals that he had designs on Kuwait. In addition to a worsening economic situation, Saddam was upset with Kuwait for drilling in the Rumayla oil fields, dangerously close to the disputed border area with Iraq. In fact, Saddam was said to believe that the Kuwaitis were taking advantage of Iraq's being bogged down in the war with Iran by taking oil from under Iraq's side of border through sophisticated, lateral drilling techniques.

Saddam Hussein also knew there was a traditional tension and competition between Saudi Arabia and Kuwait. This was due to various factors, including the fact that they were neighbors, were two of the world's major oil producers, and had taken divergent views of the role of Islam in daily life. Kuwait was known as an aggressive member of OPEC, willing to step up production and bend, if not cheat, on quotas and other agreements. Kuwait also had adopted more western practices, and discarded some of the fundamental tenets of Islam still practiced in Saudi Arabia.

Saudi Arabia was very conservative in its implementation of Islamic principles. On the oil front, it was more of a team player, strongly believing that production needed to be controlled and that prices should rise and fall gradually, as sudden changes could do lasting damage to the world economy. Some Saudis, along with other Arabs, would say that Kuwait "wasn't a country, it was an oil well." Prince Bandar, Saudi Ambassador to the United States, on his way to the bathroom, has been quoted as saying, "I have to go to the Kuwait."[1]

In foreseeing the possible need for a move against Kuwait, there is also a distinct possibility that Saddam, a master of manipulation and creation of conflict, was beginning a process of attempting to isolate Kuwait from Saudi Arabia and Bahrain.

The year 1989 was not a good one for Iraq, as falling oil prices and the foreign debt load limited the government options for dealing with the post-war recession. Within the government's constrained budget, it appeared that Saddam continued to assign a great deal of priority to military spending.

On March 17, 1990, Saddam held a little-publicized, but highly important meeting at Saudi Arabia's Hafr Al-Batin Air Force Base, near the Iraqi border, with King Fahd and Emir Jaber of Kuwait.[2]

Considering that Saddam almost never left Iraq, one could assume that the subject of the meeting was of extreme importance to him. It was. The three leaders tried to sort out the sticky question of Iraq's debt load, which had been hounding the country since the Iran-Iraq War had ended eighteen months earlier.

As Saddam probably predicted, King Fahd was willing to forgive all Saudi loans to Iraq, stating that they could be considered a gift from the Saudi people.

However, Emir Jaber said Kuwait was unable to let Iraq off the hook for billions of dollars it owed. Although the loans had been guaranteed by Kuwait, the money was loaned by western banks, mainly in the United States. The Emir offered to extend the guarantees for a while, but advised Saddam that ultimately he had to resolve the matter with the western banks from which the loans originated.

It has not been made clear how many billions of dollars were involved. Several sources said Iraq owed $10 billion to western banks by the end of its war with Iran.[3] Other sources said the actual amount Iraq needed to satisfy the payment demands was $2.8 billion.

What is clear is that Emir Jaber refused to budge, and that his obstinatness infuriated Saddam who felt all Gulf states, particularly Kuwait, owed him for defending the "neighborhood" against the Iranian aggressor.

In subsequent weeks Saddam must have become even angrier, as western bankers descended upon Baghdad to collect overdue payments of principle and interest. Again, it is difficult to show precisely why the bankers began showing up in Baghdad for collection following the March meeting at Hafr al-Batin.

One source said it was due to Kuwait's decision to "discount" its loan guarantee notes and sell them to other western banks. If this were true, it could have meant that one set of banks loaned Iraq a total of $10 billion which was guaranteed by Kuwait. Then Kuwait, fearing that Iraq's creditworthiness was in jeopardy, sold the loan guarantee notes to other western banks who had little reason to doubt the loans ultimately would be repaid. When this second set of banks smelled trouble, they went straight to Baghdad to collect.

Thus, Saddam's first attempt to ease Iraq's foreign debt burden through negotiations with Emir Jaber at Hafr Al-Batin may have only made matters worse. Even worse news for Iraq was the fact that oil prices had taken a nosedive, dropping 30 percent in the first four months of the year. Experts attributed some of the drop to cheating on production quotas by Kuwait and the United Arab Emirates.

A few weeks later, in early April 1990, four months before the invasion, King Fahd instructed Prince Bandar to fly to Baghdad to meet with Saddam Hussein. The Iraqi President told King Fahd that he wanted the Saudis to deliver a secret message to the United States.[4]

Saddam said his concern stemmed from the State Department's response to an April 3 speech in which he threatened to attack Israel. The West, Saddam had said, "will be deluded if they imagine that they can give Israel the cover to come and strike. . . By God, we will make the fire eat up half of Israel if it tries to do anything against Iraq."[5]

The State Department had called the speech "inflammatory, irresponsible, and outrageous." On April 3, 1990, the White House had issued a statement calling the remarks "particularly deplorable and irresponsible." President Bush that same day had publicly said, "This is not time to be talking about using chemical or biological weapons. This is no time to be escalating tensions in the Middle East. And I found those statements to be bad. . . . I would suggest that those statements be withdrawn."

Prince Bandar arrived in Baghdad for a private meeting with Saddam, who complained that his speech had been misunderstood and expressed regret that it was not stated differently. His real intent, Saddam told Prince Bandar, was to warn Israel against another attack, like the one Israel made on its Osirak nuclear reactor in 1981. Saddam said he had meant to threaten attack against Israel only if he were attacked. Saddam wanted to convince Prince Bandar that he did not want to be embarrassed by an Israeli attack on the eve of the Arab summit in Baghdad at the end of April.

The Iraqi President said he wanted to assure President Bush and King Fahd that he would not attack Israel. In return, he said that the Americans needed to convince Israel not to attack Iraq.[6]

In what seemed like an incongruent aside, Saddam warned Prince Bandar about the "imperialist-Zionist" conspiracy, which involved espousal of the theory that Iraq had designs over her neighbors. He denied he had any such designs.

Bandar replied that his "Arab brothers and neighbors" did not suspect him, and that since he denied it, there was no reason to worry. Saddam reportedly repeated his warning not to allow the "imperialist-Zionist" rumor mill or forces to get between us."[7]

Taking Saddam at his words, and acting upon instructions from King Fahd, Prince Bandar subsequently met with President Bush in the White House to deliver Saddam's message and secure a promise from the United States that Israel would not attack Iraq. President Bush initially declined to fulfill the request, stating only that he would think about it.

But two days later, Saddam pressured both King Fahd and the Iraqi Ambassador to Washington Mohamed Mashat to get an answer. Prince Bandar returned to the White House and finally succeeded in getting President Bush to agree that he would talk to the Israelis.

Later, the Israelis reportedly agreed not to attack Iraq first. The White House passed the message on to King Fahd, who in turn, reported it to Saddam Hussein.[8]

It is possible that Saddam seriously was worried about an Israeli attack. But there could have been a more central motive behind this extraordinary request and his persistence in securing the answer he wanted: the ability to begin moving his troops toward the Iraq-Kuwait border.

Faced with potential military threats from Iran in the east and Israel in the west, as well as the need to put down any Kurdish uprisings in the north, the Iraqi military typically was stationed close to Baghdad and central Iraq.

With the tensions lowering between Iraq and Iran, the military threat from the east was subsiding. The brutal 1988 campaign against the Kurds had kept them in check. However, Hussein appeared suddenly to become obsessed with an Israeli attack, invoking his pride and the upcoming Arab summit as principal reasons.

With the assurance that Israel would not attack, Saddam might have felt secure in shifting his offensive capabilities to the southern border with Kuwait and Saudi Arabia.

Anticipating that word might leak out about his designs on Kuwait, or that his troop movements would tip off the world that the invasion was coming, Saddam sought to preempt any concerns that might arise by alluding to any discussion of the possibility as part of the "Zionist-imperialist conspiracy."

This was a shrewd maneuver, as Arabs for years have

been the target of Israeli disinformation campaigns, and Mossad espionage, infiltration, and covert action programs. Arab suspicions of the United States run high as well, in part because it underwrites Israeli atrocities against Arabs, and because it traditionally has been well-manipulated by pro-Israeli forces.

Saddam Hussein's concern over Iraq's increasingly desperate economic situation, and his resentment toward his wealthy neighbors, suddenly surfaced at an April 28 meeting of the 21-member Arab Summit in Baghdad.

Saddam surprisingly called for a closed session restricted to the 21 heads of state. King Fahd, noting that the proposal was inconsistent with past protocol, opposed the idea, but a majority voted to hear Saddam's message.[9]

Ignoring the stated theme of the conference, which was the threat to Mideast peace posed by the emigration of Soviet Jews to Israel and their settlement in the Occupied Territories, Saddam lectured the Gulf states about their oil policies.

"They are extracting too much petrol and helping to keep prices at too low a level. Every time the price of a barrel drops by one dollar, Iraq loses $1 billion a year. You're virtually waging an economic war against my country!"[10] he said.

Saddam wanted major economic relief and he needed it fast. To drive home his point, he referred to Iraq as the "poor man" at the Arab Summit and then announced Iraq would still contribute $50 million to Jordan and $25 million to the Palestine Liberation Organization.

"That should help exert moral pressure on those who might be tempted not to contribute. You all know the sacrifices we have accepted over the years while others fail to respect their agreements," Saddam said, referring to Iraq's eighty year war with Iran.[11]

"The quotas allocated by OPEC stipulated that Kuwait should not exceed a daily production of 1.5 million barrels; in actual fact, it has constantly extracted 2.1 million barrels a day," he continued. "We are the ones to suffer. We Iraqis want to return to the economic situation that [we] obtained in 1980, before the war against Iran. For the moment we urgently need $10 billion, as well as cancellation of the $30 billion worth of debts to Kuwait, the Arab Emirates and Saudi Arabia that we incurred during the war. Indeed, brother Arabs, it has to be clearly understood that we are today living through another conflict."

As he spoke, Saddam's tone grew more violent. "War doesn't mean just tanks, artillery, or ships. It can take subtler and more insidious forms, such as the overproduction of oil, economic damage, and pressures to enslave a nation."

The surprise speech threw the meeting into an icy silence. Many Arab leaders undoubtedly saw it as more of Saddam's bravado, and an effort to shake down the richer Arab nations through idle threats and/or guilt. King Fahd, however, knew events in the region had grown dangerous in a new way. Due to his close relationship with Saddam that stemmed from supporting him throughout the Iran-Iraq War, King Fahd knew that Saddam's words could not be taken lightly. Saddam's equation of economic disagreement with hostile acts of war raised the specter that Saddam himself was pondering a military response. He also remembered that Iraq had invaded Kuwait in 1973, only to withdraw after pressure from Saudi Arabia and other Arab nations.

King Fahd believed that hostilities could be avoided through negotiations and the appropriate economic relief package. But the negotiations would have to be taken seriously and agreements reached quickly to reduce the newly enunciated tension.

While he gave his talk, Saddam directed many of his remarks to the Emir of Kuwait, Jaber Al-Sabah. Emir Jaber spoke in response to Saddam, but offered no words of encouragement and no promises of aid. In fact, the Emir seemed "strangely calm, almost indifferent" to the issues that had been raised, according to some observers.[12]   After the speech, Emir Jaber invited the Iraqi President to visit Kuwait, but Saddam, in a prophetic response, replied that he did not need an official invitation, he would be there in three months.[13]

Saddam Hussein's blustery warnings succeeded at focusing the attention of Arab heads of state on the oil issue. This was an important accomplishment, as leaving oil pricing policy to oil ministers would not have achieved the same sense of urgency. It was also consistent with Saddam's consolidating vital economic decisions at the top political level, as he did in Iraq in 1977, when he substantially enlarged his power on the Revolutionary Command Council.

The effects of Saddam's warnings were seen almost immediately. The following week in Geneva, OPEC ministers announced an agreement to cut current production by 1.4 million barrels a day in an effort to restore prices to $18 per barrel. Acting OPEC President Sadek Bousena said that countries which had been producing more than their previously agreed upon quotas would return to their ceiling levels. The United Arab Emirates, for instance, announced it would cut its output by 200,000 barrels a day, Boussena said.[14]

On May 14, Iraqi Oil Minister Issam Abdul Rahim Al-Chalabi met in Riyadh with Saudi Oil Minister Hisham Nazer. Emerging from the day-long session, Chalabi said there was now good coordination between the two countries on oil matters, including their stand in OPEC and future policy. Nazer said Saudi Arabia would adhere to the OPEC Geneva decision to keep to production quotas and effectuate a gradual raising of oil prices. He said the strategy was beginning to work. "In the beginning, market response was negative but now the prices are increasing gradually."[15]

By early June, however, progress toward raising oil prices had slowed. While production had been lowered to between 23.2 to 23.5 million barrels per day, it did not reach OPEC's Geneva goal of 22 million. This meant that prices for North Sea "Brent Blend," for instance, had only inched up to $15.50 a barrel -- far short of the $25 per barrel that Iraq wanted.[16]

Iraq's increasing economic desperation was evidenced by its invitation to some developed nations to help develop its oil fields. Japan liked the idea, and in June, proposed an "equity share" in Iraqi crude, meaning a fixed percentage of production in return for financing development projects.

But Iraq rejected any type of equity entitlements -- a system long abolished when Iraq nationalized its oil industry in 1972. Instead, Iraq insisted that repayment for investments would be in crude produced from the same fields where development took place and long-term contracts for additional supplies.

When Japanese officials visited Baghdad June 6, they apparently would not budge from their stand that it would only enter sole-risk projects if Iraq withdrew its objection to equity shares. "Japan has no oil resources and equity in this area is of vital importance to us," a Japanese official told Reuters. The talks ended with no deal. Oil competition in the Gulf remained intense, as the Japanese were able to strike a deal with Oman to operate a "concession" oil field there.

British Petroleum and Shell Oil also were exploring Iraq's offer for joint development, but no deals were ever announced.[17]

Two weeks later at the weekly meeting of the Council of Ministers in Jeddah, King Fahd reiterated his country's commitment to OPEC quotas, and, in a veiled warning to Kuwait, UAE, and other countries that reportedly were exceeding their quotas, urged all OPEC members to abide by the agreement. "It is the only way to improve and stabilize the oil market," King Fahd said, adding that adherence to quotas was "in the interest of producers as well as consumers."[18]

While there appeared a genuine effort by Saudi Arabia and some OPEC members to curb production and boost oil prices, other countries, Kuwait and United Arab Emirates in particular, continued exceeding production. By the end of June OPEC's "minimum reference" price was set at $18 a barrel but the true market price was between $14 and $15 per barrel because of the glut.

Iraq, which claimed it was losing $1 billion in desperately needed revenues for every $1 drop in the price of a barrel of oil, was not in a position to be patient.

On June 26, Iraq Deputy Prime Minister Saadoun Hammadi returned from what must have been a very unsuccessful trip aimed at convincing Emir Jaber of Kuwait and the UAE to go along with lower production and higher prices. Instead of agreeing to Iraq's plan, both Kuwait and the UAE said they wanted a bigger share of the oil market, a demand which Iraq rejected outright.

Upon returning to Baghdad, Hammadi said the price would rise to $18 per barrel from $14-$15 if only Kuwait and the UAE would agree to cut production by 1.5

million barrels per day.

To emphasize the importance of the issue and underline rejection of Kuwait and the UAE to expand their market share, Hammadi held a rare Baghdad news conference. "There should not be a review of OPEC members' quotas before a fair price is reached. In my view a fair price is definitely not below $25 a barrel, " he said.

Hammadi said that western oil consumers would be prepared to pay $25 per barrel and that this price could be achieved if OPEC members showed solidarity and restrained output. "I don't consider $25 a high price by any standard," he said.[19]

In July, much of Saudi Arabia's attention was focused on OPEC's July 25 meeting in Geneva, with a view toward responding more positively to Iraq's call for higher prices. On July 10, Saudi Oil Minister Nazer hosted a meeting of his counterparts from Iraq, Kuwait, the UAE, and Qatar to lay the groundwork for the July 25 Geneva meeting. The same day, the Associated Press reported that OPEC members continued exceeding their production quotas, and that the glut was pushing prices downward with a threat of an oil price crash similar to one that occurred in 1986.[20]

The five oil ministers emerged from the meeting and announced an agreement to give top priority to restore oil prices to more than $18 a barrel. A joint statement explained that a study would be conducted to guarantee the UAE's return and adherence to agreed allocations.[21] The next day, Nazer announced that the UAE had accepted its oil production quota of 1.5 million barrels per day, mainly because King Fahd intervened to secure agreement from UAE President Sheikh Zayed ibn Sultan Al-Nahyan.[22]

Most observers must have viewed this as a concrete

response to Iraq's continuously stated concern about low oil prices. But to Saddam Hussein, it was too little, too late. In fact, the slow-moving talks and minimal results of the Jeddah meeting of Gulf oil ministers may have convinced him that negotiations alone were not sufficient. Iraq's worsening economic situation called for more extraordinary measures, namely, the threat of force, if not the use of force.

Shortly after the Jeddah meeting, Iraq began mobilizing its military toward the Kuwait border. On July 16, U.S. intelligence satellites spotted the beginning of a brigade of an Iraqi tank division of T-72 tanks, the top-of-the-line heavy tanks supplied to Iraq by the Soviets. Satellite photos showed a variety of the elite Republican Guard's equipment being loaded on rail lines. By July 19, more than 35,000 Iraqi troops from three divisions, including the much-heralded Hammurabi division, were within ten to thirty miles from the Kuwait border.[23]

As the military began moving, Iraq stepped up its rhetoric. On July 17, for instance, Iraqi Foreign Minister Tariq Aziz gave to Chadli Klibi, Secretary-General of the Arab League, a memo which expanded Iraq's grievances against Kuwait beyond the overproduction of petroleum. Iraq accused Kuwait of installing military posts on its territory and stealing more than $2.4 billion worth of oil extracted from the Rumailah field, which Iraq claimed as its own. Kuwait and the United Arab Emirates were also named as part of a "Zionist and imperialist plot against the Arab nation." In the world of Arab diplomacy, the memo amounted to a declaration of war.[24]

The same day, Saddam Hussein, in a speech celebrating the anniversary of the Iraqi revolution, said, "Thanks to our new weapons, the imperialists can no longer launch a military attack against us, so they have chosen to wage an economic guerrilla war with the help of those agents of imperialism, the leaders of the Gulf states. Their policy of keeping oil prices at a low level is a poisoned dagger planted in Iraq's back."

In his first reference to military intervention, Saddam said, "If words fail to protect us, we will have no choice other than to go into action to reestablish the correct state of affairs and restore our rights."[25]

What Saddam wanted most urgently from the Kuwaitis was assistance in paying off debts owed to western banks and cooperation in raising oil prices. During the Iran-Iraq War, the Kuwaitis generously provided aid, reportedly giving the Iraqis 300,000 barrels of oil a day and $17 billion, but keeping the details secret out of fear of angering Iran.[26]

King Fahd saw that the situation was becoming more serious. The inability, or unwillingness, of the Kuwaitis to respond to Saddam's demands only heightened his concern. The day following Saddam's speech, Saudi Foreign Minister Prince Faisal went to Baghdad to meet with Saddam. The main purpose of Prince Faisal's meeting was to maintain dialogue so negotiations between Kuwait and Iraq could produce a settlement. The two sides agreed to a July 31 meeting in Jeddah, Saudi Arabia, hosted by King Fahd. Saddam Hussein assured Prince Faisal that Iraq had no intention of using military force against Kuwait.[27]

However, the mobilization of Iraqi troops continued at the rate of a division a day. By July 25, eight divisions had been amassed on the Kuwait border, a total of 100,000 troops.[28] There was no doubt that Iraq had the capability to exercise a military option against Kuwait. Most officials in the Gulf, though, thought that Saddam was bluffing, flexing his muscle on the eve of the OPEC

Geneva meeting so that oil prices would be raised to the long sought after price of $25 per barrel. In the worst-case scenario, officials figured that Iraq might seize the Kuwait-controlled portions of the Rumailya oil fields which straddled the two countries' borders and had been the source of continual disputes.

From Iraq's point of view, the military troop movements had the desired effect in Geneva, where Iraq continued insisting on a $25 per barrel price. On the eve of the July 25, three-day event, OPEC aides were telling the press they favored a $20 per barrel price.[29] On July 27, OPEC announced an accord raising the target price from $18 to $21. The announcement prompted oil prices to rise from $16.25 the previous week to nearly $20 on the market.

Iranian Oil Minister Gholam Reza Aqazadeh said he was confident the production quotas this time would be strictly enforced, as the OPEC agreement was reached at the "highest levels of the OPEC governments." The Associated Press reported, "In reaching the agreement, the ministers persuaded Iraqi Minister Issam Abdul Raheem Al-Chalabi to back off his demand for a $25 a barrel target price. Others said $25 was too high."[30]

This was not enough for Saddam Hussein, who continued sending signals that he was seriously considering a military invasion of Kuwait if the direct negotiations scheduled for Jeddah did not promptly produce the relief he sought.

With his military forces almost ready, Saddam knew that there was nothing that could physically stop his army from taking any or all of Kuwait if the ruling Sabah family failed to give into his demands. He more than likely believed that King Fahd was too slow-moving, indecisive, and short of courage to stand up to him, and that the Saudi ruler, who he perceived as preferring the path of least resistance, may even have agreed to divide the spoils once Kuwait was under Iraqi control. If King Fahd chose to oppose Iraq, he knew that Saudi Arabia had devoted its military build up to air power, and that the Saudi army was no match for the Iraqi army. He also knew that the other regional power, Iran, would never come to Kuwait's rescue.

What might have been most difficult for Iraq's ruling council was predicting how the United States would respond to a move against Kuwait. All indications are that Saddam Hussein felt that America's distaste for war ultimately would preclude it from mounting a major military operation on behalf of Kuwait, a country thousands of miles away. Moreover, he might have thought that President Bush, who had ordered the invasion of a tiny neighbor, Panama, because of his grudge against Manuel Noreiga, would understand how Saddam could have lost his patience with the arrogant Kuwaitis.

On the other hand, Saddam had some cause for concern. The United States had moved relatively quickly in the mid-1980s to protect Kuwaiti tankers from attacks in the Iran-Iraq War. Bush too spent many years in the oil industry and knew the importance of Kuwait to the world's oil supply.

Perhaps seeking to confirm his view that the United States would not risk its own soldiers to save Kuwait, Saddam Hussein, on July 25, suddenly summoned April Glaspie, U.S. Ambassador to Iraq, for a surprise, four-hour meeting Ignoring the apparent progress on oil prices, he repeated to her the description of economic desperation he imparted to Arab leaders a few months earlier.

"We believe that the United States must understand that people who live in luxury and economic security can reach an understanding with the United States about what are legitimate joint interests, but the starved and the economically deprived cannot reach the same understanding."

Similarly, he asserted that Iraq was the one that restored stability to the region by beating back Iran. He acknowledged the United States' desire for the secure flow of oil, but warned it to stop encouraging "some parties to harm Iraq's interest" and not to resort to "the flexing of muscles and pressure." He added: "If you use pressure, we will deploy both pressure and force."

Saddam conceded Iraq could not invade the United States, but implied that terrorists could do damage there. Iraq, he explained, would rather fight than submit to outside pressures.

"You can come to Iraq with aircraft and missiles, but do not push us to the point at which we cease to care. When we feel that you want to injure our pride and destroy the Iraqis' chance of a high standard of living, we will cease to care, and death will be our choice. Then we would not care if you fired a hundred missiles for each missile we fired because, without pride, life would have no value."

Continuing his lecture, Saddam said his most immediate problem was the economic pressure from Kuwait. It is not reasonable to ask our people to bleed rivers of blood for eight years, then to tell them, "Now you have to accept aggression from Kuwait, the UAE, the U.S., or Israel."

He continued to express concern over the possibility of an Israeli attack, citing the Israel Defense Minister's presence in Washington and the "fiery statements" coming out of Israel.

Saddam said he hoped that the United States would not push Iraq to the point that it reached with Iran. He did not remind Glaspie that when "at that point" with Iran in 1980, Iraq invaded.

When Glaspie finally was able to respond, she said, "I clearly understand your message. We study history at school. They taught us to say, 'Freedom or death.' I think you know well that we as a people have our own experience of colonialists."

She went on to explain that she had direct instruction from President Bush to seek better relations with Iraq. Saddam asked, "How?" Glaspie said continued negotiations was the best way.

Saddam, however, said a campaign against him by the U.S. media continued unabated.

Glaspie agreed there was such a campaign intended to harm him.

"I saw the Diane Sawyer program on ABC," said the Iraqi President. "And what happened in that program was cheap and unjust. And this is a real picture of what happens in the American media -- even to American politicians themselves. These are the methods that the Western media employ. I am pleased that you add your voice to the diplomats who stand up to the media because your appearance in the media, even for five minutes, could help us to make the American people understand Iraq. This would increase mutual understanding. If the American President had control of the media, his job would be much easier."

Glaspie responded, "Mr. President, I want to say that President Bush wants not only better and deeper relations with Iraq but also an Iraqi contribution to peace and prosperity in the Middle East. President Bush is an intelligent man. He is not going to declare an economic war against Iraq."

Saddam continued, "You are right. It is true what you say that we do not want higher prices for oil. But I would ask you to examine the possibility of not charging too high a price for oil."

The two sides began focusing on the all-important details. Iraqi Foreign Minister Tariq Aziz said his country's policy opposed sudden jumps in oil prices. Saddam added, "Twenty-five dollars a barrel is not a high price."

Still conciliatory, Glaspie said, "We have many Americans who would like to see the price go above $25 because they come from oil-producing states." Knowing Bush too was from an oil-producing state, Saddam most likely interpreted this as a green light for maintaining higher oil prices.

"The price at one stage had dropped to $12 a barrel, and a reduction in the modest Iraqi budget of $6 to 7 billion is a disaster," Saddam said.

Glaspie, in perhaps her most famous moment, responded: "I think I understand this. I have lived here for years. I admire your extraordinary efforts to rebuild your country. I know you need funds. We understand that, and our opinion is that you should have the opportunity to rebuild your country. But we have no opinion on Arab-Arab conflicts, like your border disagreement with Kuwait."

"I was in the American Embassy in Kuwait during the late 1960s. The instruction we had during that period was that we should express no opinion on this issue and that the issue was not associated with America. James Baker has directed our official spokesman to emphasize this instruction. We hope you can solve this problem using any suitable methods via Kalibi [Secretary-General of the Arab League] or President Mubarak. With regard to all of this, can I ask you to understand how the issue appears to us?"

Though open to different interpretation, Glaspie's

question could be seen implying again that the situation was an Arab-Arab affair that did not concern the United States.

She continued: "Frankly, we can see only that you have deployed massive troops in the south. Normally that would not be any of our business. But when this happens in the context of what you said on your National Day, when we read the details in the two letters of the Foreign Minister, when we see the Iraqi point of view that the measure taken by the UAE and Kuwait are, in the final analysis, tantamount to military aggression against Iraq, then it is reasonable for me to be concerned. And for this reason I have received an instruction to ask you, in the spirit of friendship, not in the spirit of confrontation, about your intentions."

Saddam was not about to answer such a direct question directly. He first said he wanted to find a "just solution," and that Iraq had been cooperating with OPEC efforts organized by the Saudis. While it appeared an agreement had been worked out, Saddam claimed that he learned the Kuwaitis were about to renege.

"Now tell us: If the American President found himself in this situation, what would he do?," possibly thinking of recent U.S. invasions of Grenada and Panama for different reasons.

"I said it was very difficult for me to talk about these issues in public. But we must tell the Iraqi people, who face economic difficulties, who was responsible for that."

This time Glaspie avoided answering directly and changed the subject by mentioning the four beautiful years she spent in Egypt. Then she tried again, asking Saddam to assess Arab efforts to broker the current dispute.

To Glaspie's relief, Saddam explained that the

Saudis had initiated contact with him and, with the help of President Mubarak of Egypt, had arranged an Iraqi-Kuwaiti meeting in Jeddah, to be followed by a meeting in Baghdad to focus on details. "We hope that the long-term view and the real interests at stake will overcome Kuwaiti greed," Saddam said, pointing out that Sheikh Saad was expected to come to Baghdad on July 28 or 30.

"This is good news. Congratulations," responded Glaspie.

But Saddam warned her the potential for disaster was still great.

"Brother President Mubarak told me they were scared. They said troops were only 20 kilometers north of the Arab League line [the Kuwaiti border]. I said to him that regardless of what is there, whether they are police border guards, or army, and regardless of how many are there and what they are doing, assure the Kuwaitis and given them our word that we are not going to do anything until we meet with them. If, when we meet, we see that there is hope, nothing will happen. But if we are unable to find a solution, then it will be natural that Iraq will not accept death, even though wisdom is above everything else. There your have good news."

"This is a journalistic exclusive," chipped in Tariq Aziz, attempting to underscore the importance of Saddam's warning in terms an American could understand.

But Glaspie only appeared to have retained the optimistic messages, while filtering out the more important advisories. Vowing to take the message to Bush, she said, "I am planning to go to the United States next Monday [July 30]. I hope I will meet with President Bush in Washington next week. I thought to postpone my trip because of the difficulties we are facing. But now I will fly on Monday."[31]

Given that this was Glaspie's first private meeting with Saddam, perhaps it was understandable that she appeared to miss the vital warning signs that he had given. What she failed to understand was that Saddam basically had spent five months trying to "negotiate" away his economic problems, and that whatever patience he might have had for the process had evaporated. He was probing her to confirm that the United States' interest in Kuwait was not so great that it would commit to a major military operation if Kuwait were invaded. Glaspie's comment that the U.S. had no position on "Arab-Arab" disputes while 100,000 Iraqi troops were amassing on the Kuwaiti border, at minimum bolstered Saddam's view there were no real restraints. Saddam undoubtedly came away from the meeting believing just that. As one western diplomat put it, "I don't for a minute think that Glaspie's meeting was dispositive to the Gulf War. But sending her in to see Saddam at that point in time was probably the wrong signal. [The U.S.] should have sent in a street thug and made it clear we were ready to fight."[32]

King Fahd still took the situation very seriously. He understood that Emir Jaber was not planning to attend his Jeddah summit, but he tried to convince him that the Kuwaiti delegation should approach the meeting in the spirit of compromise. The day after the Saddam-Glaspie meeting, July 26, King Fahd wrote a letter to the Emir of Kuwait, stressing the importance of his leading the Kuwaiti delegation to the Jeddah summit.

"At a time when I am looking forward to this brotherly meeting, may I point out how fully confident I am that your wisdom and foresight will, God willing, achieve our aims, our brother Arabs: to reduce all difficulties and to ensure the love and understanding between two sisterly states."[33]

But the Emir's response highlighted his rather suspicious and inflexible nature. In a note to his brother he wrote on King Fahd's letter, he said: "We should be present at the meeting under the same previously agreed upon conditions. It is noteworthy for us to keep in mind our national interests; therefore don't listen to whatever you may hear from the Saudis or Iraqis in regard to brotherhood and maintaining Arab solidarity. Each has his own interests to cater to. The Saudis want to weaken us and to exploit our concessions to the Iraqis so that we will make concessions to them in the demilitarized zone. As for the Iraqis, they wish to compensate for the cost of their war from our resources. Neither demand will bear fruit . . . that is also the position of our friends in Egypt, Washington, and London. We wish you good luck."[34]

These thoughts, of course, stayed within the Kuwaiti ruling circle. The Emir wrote back to King Fahd thanking him for his invitation, telling him he would be represented by his brother and sounding highly optimistic about the Jeddah meeting. "May I also thank and commend your brotherly effort, wisdom, and guidance and support will, God willing, lead to beneficent results, the reduction of all difficulties and the mutual confidence and love to all."[35]

In the days leading to the Jeddah summit, events began moving very quickly. On July 28, Saddam Hussein told PLO Chief Yasser Arafat in Baghdad that he should go to Kuwait and tell the Emir that if he gave Saddam several billion dollars as payment for use of the Rumailah oil wells on the border, Saddam would reduce his troops. But when Arafat arrived in Kuwait City, the Emir rejected the proposal.[36]

At some point before the summit, King Fahd told

the Emir that Saudi Arabia would pay several billions of dollars the Iraqis were demanding from Kuwait. But the Emir refused to allow it, stating that Iraq was trying to blackmail Kuwait and that if the Saudis paid it this time, the Iraqis would come back for more again and again.[37]

July 30, the eve of the Jeddah summit, John Kelly, Assistant Secretary of State, was being questioned by a House Foreign Affairs subcommittee about the buildup of Iraqi troops on the Kuwaiti border.

Rep. Lee Hamilton asked, "Defense Secretary Richard Cheney has been quoted in the press as saying that the United States was committed to going to the defense of Kuwait if she were attacked. Is that exactly what was said? Could Mr. Kelly clarify this?"

Kelly said the United States was committed to the independence, stability, and sovereignty of Gulf nations, and to the peaceful resolution of all disputes. However, he said, "We don't have any defense treaty with the Gulf states. That's clear."

Hamilton pressed him about the specific possibility of Iraqi troops crossing the Kuwaiti border. Kelly said he could not comment on hypothetical situations.

"If such a thing should happen, though, is it correct to say that we have no treaty, no commitment, which would oblige us to use American forces?" Hamilton persisted.

"That's exactly right," Kelly replied.

Kelly's statements were broadcast on the World Service of the BBC and were heard in Baghdad. As Pierre Salinger, the ABC News correspondent put it, "At a crucial hour, when war and peace hung in the balance, Kelly had sent Saddam Hussein a signal that could be read as a pledge that the United States would not intervene. In the recent history of American diplomacy there had been only one other example of such a serious miscalculation, and that was Secretary of State Dean Acheson's statement to Congress in 1950 that 'South Korea was not part of the United States' zone of defense. Soon afterwards, North Korea had invaded the South."[38]

Salinger may assign more importance to Kelly's words than may be justified, just as others had heaped all the blame on Glaspie. But taken together the two statement did nothing to discourage Saddam from going ahead with the invasion.

On July 30, three Iraqi officials left Baghdad for the ill-fated Jeddah meeting where they were to meet a Kuwaiti delegation and continue the negotiation.

The Jeddah summit took place amidst a gloomy and threatening backdrop. First, both the animosity which Saddam Hussein and the Emir of Kuwait had for each other was boiling over, and neither were about to authorize its delegation to "give into" the other. Second, the Iraqi Army was poised at the border and ready to invade. The United States continued to miscalculate Saddam's intentions and then add fuel to the fire by sending signals it would not get involved if there was an invasion.

The Jeddah summit was scheduled to last through August 1, but the real action took place the first evening, July 31. Crown Prince Abdallah, second-ranking official in the Saudi Kingdom, welcomed the two delegations and left them alone so they could commence negotiations.

Although there's no authoritative record available about what went on in the meeting, some reports of it appear fairly reliable. The key details are not in dispute: the Iraqis and Kuwaitis could not come to an agreement over how much money, if any, Kuwait would pay to Iraq for oil it took from the Rumayla oil field; the discussions lasted several hours and grew quite heated at times, with the Kuwaiti delegation making statements that the Iraqis took as insults; and all sides agreed there would be a second meeting in Baghdad in three days.

Sources confirmed that the two sides came to Jeddah in no mood to compromise. The Kuwaitis, seeking to disprove Iraqi claims that they had taken oil from Iraq's side of the border, came with a coterie of legal, topological, and petroleum expert witnesses. The Iraqis, on the hand, came only to present to the Kuwaitis "a bottom line" which they could either sign--or face the consequences.

After the first few hours, it was clear to neutral observers waiting outside that the Kuwaitis were not happy with the way the meeting was going, and increasingly were showing their irritation as they scurried in and out of the meeting.

According to Salinger, Izzat Ibrahim, the second-ranking Ba'ath Party official who was sent in Saddam's place, read a long list of grievances against Kuwait. Crown Prince Saad refuted each grievance one by one.[39] Salinger reported that negotiations came to an impasse when the Iraqis demanded $10 billion and the Kuwaitis would only offer $9 billion. Authoritative Saudi sources, however, disputed that the two sides even got this close to an agreement.

After breaking for prayers, the delegations returned to a dinner meeting hosted by King Fahd, and joined by King Hussein and Abdullah Bishara, Kuwaiti Secretary of the Gulf Cooperation Council. Salinger wrote that King Fahd broke an impasse by offering to pay to Iraq the $1 billion that separated the two sides. Again, Saudi sources deny that this account, but agreed on an earlier date when the King had offered to pay billions of dollars which Iraq claimed was owed to it by Kuwait, but that

Emir Jaber, calling it blackmail, would not allow it. Finally, Salinger writes that after King Fahd and King Hussein retired for the evening, the Iraqis and Kuwaitis, like unruly children with parents out of sight, were arguing again over money and borders. It was at the end of the evening when the Kuwaiti insults started flying and the Iraqis warned them that their days as an independent nation were numbered.

Clearly, though, King Fahd and King Hussein of Jordan left the dinner with the belief that they had achieved their goal of keeping the lines of communications open between the Iraqis and the Kuwaitis and heading off a disagreement that could have exploded into something much worse.[40] The two hoped that the upcoming meeting in Baghdad would lead to a final resolution of differences.

The next day, August 1, the Iraqis rejected a Kuwaiti proposal to put out a joint communique. The Kuwaiti delegation left Jeddah around 4:00 p.m. The Kuwaitis, along with other Arabs, thought there would be another chance, as it already had been agreed that negotiations would resume in Baghdad August 3, and that this session would be the one that would deal with the sticky details that led to the heated argument between the two delegations.

The Iraqis knew differently, however. They left Jeddah around noon on August 1, without saying farewell to or thanking their host King Fahd, an immense transgression in Arab culture. By the time the delegation arrived in Baghdad, Saddam Hussein might already have decided to invade Kuwait. Either way, the offensive would begin that night.[41]

In the final days before the invasion, it seems likely that the more Saddam Hussein thought about taking Kuwait the more he liked it. First, he saw no evidence that the Saudis had the capability, or the United States had the will, to defend Kuwait. Second, seizing Kuwait would help solve Iraq's short-term economic problems by simultaneously doubling its oil supply and driving up the price of oil. Third, it would leave him in a strong bargaining position to at least gain more of the Rumayla oil field as well as the two islands in the Gulf so Iraq finally would secure its own warm water port.

It is also important to mention that Saddam saw a much larger payoff in invading Kuwait. As his history reveals, the man was motivated not only by the egocentric goal of becoming a Nasser-like leader of the pan-Arab world, but one of the most powerful figures in the entire world. This motivation was central to his poorly conceived invasion of Iran.

The ticket to becoming a world power was economic wealth, a large army, and nuclear force. The Iraqi army was rated the fourth-largest in the world. In addition, Saddam had developed strong ties to terrorists like Abu Nidal, and could always invoke the threat of terrorism for geopolitical gain. Iraq was closing in on its nuclear bomb, and was on the verge of joining the world's select nuclear club.

The last hurdle was economics. Kuwait's oil fields were the answer to that problem. And if Iraq could take Kuwait, it could also consider seizing the United Arab Emirates' rich oil reserves and maybe even the nearby Eastern Province of Saudi Arabia.

Saddam probably saw that he was one invasion away from becoming an economic power which, along with his military and soon-to-be unveiled nuclear capability, would make him an undisputed world power, dominating one of the most important regions in the world.

1. Woodward, Bob. *The Commanders.*
2. *Arab News,* March 18, 1990.
3. Souresrafil, Behrouz. *The Iran-Iraq War,* Guinan Lit. Co., Plainview, NY, pg. 135 or Salinger, Pierre & Laurent, Eric. *Secret Cossier.*
4. *The Commanders.* pgs. 199-202.
5. Ibid.
6. Ibid.
7. Ibid.
8. Ibid., pg. 204.
9. Salinger, Pierre. *Secret Dossier: The Hidden Agenda Behind The Gulf War,* Penguin Books, 1991, pg. 29.
10. Ibid., pg. 30.
11. Ibid., pg. 31.
12. Ibid., pg. 32.
13. Confidential sources.
14. *Arab News,* April 5, 1990.
15. *Arab News,* May 15, 1990.
16. *Arab News,* June 5, 1990.
17. *Arab News,* June 5, 1990.
18. *Arab News,* June 19, 1991.
19. *Arab News,* June 27, 1990.
20. *Arab News,* July 11, 1990.
21. *Arab News,* July 12, 1990.
22. *Arub News,* July 13, 1990.
23. *The Commanders.* pgs. 206-207.
24. Ibid., pg. 39.
25. Ibid., pg. 40.
26. Ibid., pg. 40.
27. Confidential sources.
28. *The Commanders.* pg. 210.
29. *Arab News,* July 26, 1991.
30. *Arab News,* July 28, 1991.
31. Saddam-Glaspie transcript.

74

32. Based on interviews.
33. Ibid., pg. 64.
34. Ibid., pg. 65.
35. Ibid., pg. 65.
36. Ibid., pg. 68.
37. Confidential sources.
38. Ibid., pg. 69.
39. Ibid., pg. 72.
40. Ibid., pg. 75.
41. Ibid., pg. 77.

4

AFTER THE INVASION

King Fahd was awakened at around 5:00 a.m. and informed of Iraq's invasion of Kuwait immediately after confirmations of it reached Saudi Arabia. In all of his years leading the kingdom, as well as the previous period heading various governmental ministries, this may have been the most surprising and shocking news he ever heard. He had thought that the Jeddah summit had substantially closed the gap between the Iraqis and Kuwaitis. More important, they were scheduled to resume talks in Baghdad in two days.

King Fahd would have been more shocked had he known that Iraqi paratroopers had contingency plans for landing in the United Arab Emirates and seizing their oil fields. The plan involved leapfrogging the stretch of Saudi territory bordering the Gulf between Kuwait and the UAE, and setting up fortified positions in the UAE. This would have enabled the Iraqis to effectively encircle the oil-rich Dharan section of the Eastern Province, placing them in a perfect position to seize them next if they so chose.[1]

As one western diplomat explained: "Saddam learned from his mistaken invasion of Iran that he could not just rush into Kuwait, the Eastern Province, and UAE all at once. He realized that he needed to approach the region like a good burglar approaches a wealthy neighborhood: you burgle the first house, and if you don't get caught you move on to the next one and the next, until the dangers outweigh the benefits"[2]

Lacking this vital data, King Fahd first wanted to speak with Saddam Hussein. While it appears naive with the benefit of hindsight, King Fahd at that moment found it difficult to believe that Saddam would deceive him in light of eight years of Saudi support during the Iran-Iraq War and his recent efforts to mediate the dispute.

But when he tried to call Saddam Hussein directly, he could not get through, undoubtedly because Saddam was in his highly secure war situation room and out of reach. He then awoke King Hussein of Jordan with an early morning call, informing him that the Iraqi Army had crossed the border and was within a few miles of Kuwait City. He requested that King Hussein contact Saddam and seek the withdrawal of the Iraqi Army to the disputed border region.

King Hussein promised to intervene at once. But he too was unable to reach Saddam immediately in his war bunker.[3]

King Fahd's call to King Hussein set off a chain of efforts by Arab leaders to continue negotiations aimed at halting, and ultimately reversing, Iraq's invasion. Such negotiations would contain resolution of the dispute in the Arab world and preclude the need for assistance or intervention by outside forces. King Fahd initially had great faith in prospects for Arab diplomacy, as it had deterred an Iraqi incursion into Kuwait in 1973. Moreover, one of the firmest principles of Saudi policy was the prohibition against the presence of non-Islamic troops in the Kingdom, where Makkah and Madinah, Islam's two holiest places, are located.

The Iraqi army achieved an immediate victory. Iraqi

tanks made it to Kuwait City in three and one half hours. The looting of the city quickly folowed, and pleas for help from Kuwaitis resisting the invasion were broadcast on short-wave radios. Iraqi radio announced that some little-known Kuwaiti nationalist had seized power and "invited" the Iraqis to enter Kuwait, a transparent play that was curiously similar to one used by the Central Intelligence Agency when it over threw the elected government of Jacobo Arbenz in Guatemala in 1954 and installed its puppet, Castillo Armas.

Moreover, Iraq took over Kuwait's oil fields, an estimated 10 percent of the world supply and potential oil profits of $20 million per day. In one morning, Iraq effectively had doubled its control over the world's oil supply. The price of oil on the world markets began to soar.

About seven hours later, at 1:00 p.m., King Hussein was able to reach Saddam, who promptly assured the Jordanian leader of his intention to begin within days a withdrawal that would take a few weeks. Convinced that a quick negotiated settlement was possible, King Hussein prepared to fly to Baghdad to meet with Saddam. Hussein wanted to organize an Arab "mini-summit" in Jeddah, Saudi Arabia in two days, August 4.

Prior to flying to Baghdad, King Hussein asked President Mubarak of Egypt to call King Fahd and other Arab leaders and ask them to refrain from making hostile statements or taking sides for the next forty-eight hours. King Fahd agreed.[4] King Hussein also asserted that he gained the Bush Administration's agreement to give him forty-eight hours to work out an Arab solution.

About the same time ministers to the Arab League in Cairo attended a hastily arranged meeting. While the Kuwaiti delegation demanded the immediate implementation of the Arab defense pact that called on all Arab nations to defend against attacks on a member, with the exception of the United Arab Emirates, most of the countries expressed a "wait-and-see" attitude in the hope that it would facilitate a diplomatic solution.

Saudi Foreign Minister Prince Saud al-Faisal, for instance spoke of the warm friendship that existed between King Fahd and Saddam Hussein. "Saudi Arab is not in accord with the invasion of Kuwait, but we are presuaded that Saddam will pull out."[5]

Some ten hours after the invasion began, King Fahd finally got through to Saddam Hussein. Stalling for time in order to consolidate his control over Kuwait and maintain his option for moves against the UAE and Saudi Arabia, Saddam said the incursion into Kuwait was only an exercise. He said it was better to not discuss details over the phone, and that he would send an envoy tomorrow to meet with the King.

Hoping that the situation could be salvaged, the Saudi government refrained from issuing any statements to the press criticizing the invasion. The headline in the next day's (Aug. 3) *Arab News* read, "Fahd Strives to Ease Iraq-Kuwait Tension."

That night in Cairo, however, Iraqi Deputy Prime Minister Saddoum Hammadi put a damper on hopes for successful Arab diplomacy with a speech that accused "certain Arab nations" of entering into an economic conspiracy against Iraq by maintaining low oil prices. His speech lacked even a hint of concession, and charged that the Gulf states were ungrateful for the shield that Iraq had provided them against Iran. Hammadi's address stunned the Arab diplomats, as he effectively poured a cold bucket of water on their hopes for a peaceful solution.

The morning of August 3, King Hussein arrived in Baghdad for talks with Saddam. The Iraqi President reportedly said he intended to withdraw from any condemnations of his invasion from Arab League members. A few hours after the meeting, Saddam Hussein issued a communique announcing that he would begin to withdraw his troops from Kuwait on Sunday, August 5. But the communique did not address the status of the Emir or his regime. More important, Saddam's troops showed no sign of withdrawing. In fact, some of the army were solidifying their positions while others appeared to be advancing toward the Saudi border.

Later on August 3, President Bush called King Fahd to share the latest intelligence, which the President said indicated the Iraqi army was in position to march on Saudi Arabia. Bush promised to support the Kingdom if the situation worsened.

King Fahd said he was still reserving judgment on the appropriate response. He said King Hussein's efforts for an Arab solution had to be given a chance, and that the Arab mini-summit was due to be held the following day, August 4. The Saudis were chosen to mediate the all-important summit. In the meantime, he had ordered Prince Bandar, the Saudi Ambassador to Washington, to fly from Europe to Washington to meet with Bush.

Shortly thereafter, Ibrahim arrived from Iraq for his meeting on behalf of Saddam. Ibrahim shocked the King by telling him that Kuwait is part of Iraq and the "branch had returned to the root." Noting the discrepency between Ibrahim's statement and Saddam's initial claim that the invasion was an "exercise," King Fahd, in disbelief asked, "Is this the message you have for me from Saddam?" "Yes," Ibrahim replied. King Fahd abruptly ended the meeting.[6]

The Bush Administration, which was caught completely by surprise by the invasion, was frantically working to orchestrate worldwide condemnation of Iraq. It had succeeded in advocating condemnations by the United Nations and the European Community. However, the Arab governments' mild reaction to the invasion as expressed in the August 3 Cairo meeting, coupled with the wait-and-see attitude expressed by King Fahd, clearly had the Bush Administration worried that the Arabs would opt for appeasement, rather than confrontation.

Unnamed American officials told the *New York Times* that they did not believe the Jordanians' explanation that the refrain from condemning Iraq's invasion was to keep alive the hope for a mediated settlement. These officials said they believed King Hussein has "simply thrown his lot with Saddam Hussein" and expressed fear that King Fahd of Saudi Arabia would be willing to pay a high price for peace.[7]

"Imagine," one American official said, "that Saddam comes to them (the Gulf Arabs) and says 'I would love to get out of Kuwait, but I just can't get out and let the Sabahs come back. How could I explain that at home? I can't be embarrassed like that.' Our answer would be, 'You put yourself in this fix, you figure it out.' But the Gulf Arabs might use that as an opening to say, O.K. just get out of Kuwait and promise you won't threaten us. You can leave behind whatever regime you want."

One "senior American official" explained to New York Times reporter Thomas L. Friedman that the Saudis were trying to juggle "three different impulses: to avoid appearing proactive to Iraq, to give time for Arab mediation to convince the Iraqis to pull back and for self-protection."

"The Saudis are being the Saudis," the official continued. "They want us there to save them one second before the Iraqis invade and not a moment sooner. We know that they would like us to go beat up Iraq, then they can come out and condemn us and then go home and thank Allah 80 million times for what we did."

The bitter and condescending tone of the "senior American official" reflected the Bush Administration's disappointment that the Arab world was respecting King Hussein's forty-eight hour deadline to achieve the Iraqi army's withdrawal from Kuwait. The Americans' unhappiness was channelled into an intense effort to pressure Arab governments, in particular Egyptian President Hosni Mubarak, to condemn the Iraqis.

The decision to focus on Mubarak was effective, as the U.S. State Department knew that Egypt, which has a $7.1 billion dollar debt with the American government, would have to listen to its primary creditor.

On the afternoon of August 3, with Egypt leading the charge at the Cairo meeting, foreign ministers at the Arab League voted 14-7 to condemn the invasion and call for Iraq's unconditional withdrawal. The resolution had the effect of cancelling the next day's mini-summit in Jeddah, as Saddam Hussein only agreed to attend if Iraq's actions were not condemned. King Hussein later would say that Mubarak had broken the forty-eight hour, no-condemnation agreement, due mainly to United States pressure that was designed to sabotage an Arab peace plan.

To date, King Hussein expresses the view that the entire war could have been avoided by proceeding to the Jeddah summit, because Saddam Hussein would have agreed to pull out in exchange for Kuwaiti and United Arab Emirates' promises to settle disputes over oil and debts. He disputed claims that Saddam had any intention of invading Saudi Arabia.

However, critics countered that King Hussein was too naive about Saddam's true intentions or worse -- was part of a conspiracy theory; Iraq would seize the oil-rich Eastern Province, Yemen would take the southern part of the Kingdom which it traditionally had claimed as its own, and King Hussein would be come the ruler of Makkah and Madinah, the two holiest sites in the Islamic world. After all, King Hussein was a descendant of the Prophet Mohammad.

What is overlooked by many is that the resolution adopted that fateful day also called for western powers not to deploy any troops on Arab soil, a clause that was supported by Saudi Arabia, Egypt and Syria.

But increasingly, Saudi attention was focused less upon diplomatic resolutions and more upon the fact that major portions of the 100,000 man Iraqi army were advancing toward the Saudi border. In fact, the Iraqi forces in Kuwait were being resupplied and reorganized some ten miles from the Saudi border.

In contrast, the Saudi army had only 70,000 men; only a Saudi National Guard unit of fewer than 1,000 men stood between several Iraqi battallions, the Saudi Kingdom, and its rich oil fields.

The numbers in the air were not much better. Iraq had 1,127 aircraft, though only with limited quantities of the most modern Soviet- and French-made fighters. The Saudis had sixty U.S.-supplied F-15s and 115 older F-5s. Tornado jet fighters ordered from Great Britian were not operational.

The threat to Saudi sovereignty was obvious. Although the Kingdom had invested billions of dollars in its defense, its defense plan was focused on repelling an air attack from Israel. Hence the emphasis on a quality air force, the most expensive arm of the military, over the development of large-scale ground forces, artillery, and tanks. Saudi defense planners simply did not envision an invasion by an Arab neighbor like Saddam.

Considering that control of oil production was a major Iraqi goal, it had even more incentives to invade Saudi Arabia. The Saudi fields comprise some 20 percent of the world's oil supply, and recent research indicates the percentage may turn out to be much higher. This meant that Saddam's armies were within miles of suddenly controlling 40 percent of the world's oil supply.

The prospect of Saddam emerging as kingpin of the oil world sent shudders through much of the world's political and commercial centers. Experts quickly pointed out that the oil crises of the 1970s sent the economies of the United States and several western nations into a recession from which it took years to escape. A severe disruption in the flow of Middle East oil could plunge the world into a depression, experts warned.

The Bush White House was very aware of the implicatons the invasion had for the economic health of the western world, and was in no mood to wait for Arab diplomacy or anything else. Administration officials were moving quickly on several fronts. They were applying pressure to Egypt and the Arab League to condemn the invasion. They were reviewing military options. They were pulling together economic forecasts

But the key concern to the United States was Saudi Arabia. With its vast oil resources and strategic location, the loss of Saudi Arabia to Saddam Hussein would allow the Iraqi President to wreak immediate havoc on the world economy.

Prince Bandar, the Saudi Ambassador to the United States, rushed back to Washington from Europe, a meeting was arranged for him, President Bush and National Security Advisor Brent Scowcroft in the White House.

Scowcroft started the meeting alone with Prince Bandar and said he was speaking for the President. He informed the Ambassador that the Saudi government had not responded to the U.S. offer of a squadron of F-15s. Understanding this non-response to mean "no" for the moment, Scowcroft said President Bush wanted to do more, and was "inclined to help in any way possible."[8]

Bandar was skeptical. He reminded Scowcroft that only a decade before when the Shah of Iran had fallen from power, President Carter has asked Saudi permission to send squadrons of F-15s to Saudi Arabia as a gesture, to which the King agreed. When the planes were half way to the region, Carter announced they were unarmed. And this was only one experience that dampened Saudi trust for U.S. leaders. As a student of the U.S. system, Prince Bandar understood that the American style of democracy not only constrains a president's ability to make commitments, but also to stand by the commitment he makes if they later prove unpopular with Congress, the media, or the public.

He told Scowcroft frankly that the Saudis were worried about the U.S. commitment and resolve. "We don't want you to put out a hand and then pull it back, and leave us with this guy on our border twice as mad as he is now," Bandar said.[9]

Scowcroft assured Bandar the U.S. would stand by its words, but said the Saudis too had to show the United States it was ready to do its part.

President Bush joined the meeting, and told the Ambassador he was concerned the Saudis, like the Kuwaitis, would only ask for military help after it was too late.

Bandar said he needed to know precisely what kind of help could be provided. How many aircraft? What sort of weapons? Only with these data could King Fahd make the corrrect decision, he told them. Bush and Scowcroft said defense Secretary Richard Cheney and Colin Powell, chairman of the Joint Chiefs of Staff, would provide a detailed briefing.

But Bandar had to satisfy himself that the United States was ready this time. He probed President Bush's resolve by repeating the story about President Carter and the unarmed F-15s.

Bush looked him in the eye and said, "I give my word of honor. I will see this through with you."

That afternoon, Bandar met with Defense Secretary Cheney and Colin Powell, who vowed the U.S. commitment was very serious and that an operations plan called "90-1002" entailed the movement of three aircraft carriers, several attack squadrons and between 100,000 and 200,000 troops into the theater. Bandar agreed the plan was a good one, and demonstrated U.S. seriousness.

Then Cheney produced high resolution satellite photographs showing Iraqi divisions advancing through Kuwait toward the Saudi border. Not only was the U.S. intelligence of vital importance to Saudi Arabia, the fact that the two highest ranking U.S. military officials personally were sharing it with him demonstrated the Bush Administration's seriousness. The operation plan was the most highly classified Pentagon document concerning the defense of the Gulf, the region considered by the United States to be one of the most important, if not the most important in the world. Bandar also knew that the United States jealously guards satellite intelligence photos, as revealing them, even to allies, risks exposure of vital intelligence gathering methods. Jonathon Pollard, the American convicted of spying for Israel, worked hard to steal many such satellite photos of the Middle East from the U.S. Navy.

The satellite photos were dramatic. They showed three Iraqi armored divisions which had led the thrust into Kuwait. One already was moving through Kuwait to the Saudi border; the others appeared ready to follow. Still more Iraqi divisions were taking places behind the armored units in the same way they had before the invasion of Kuwait two days earlier. The streak of divisions looked like a sword pointing down at the Saudi Kingdom.[10]

The Saudis were concerned prior to Bandar's meeting with Administraton officials. Not only were Saddam Hussein and his officials not being candid with King Fahd about their intentions, but there also had been three serious incursions by the Iraqis at the Saudi border since the invasion had begun forty-eight hours ago.

After the first incident, a Saudi military officer, using a hotline telephone installed during the Iran-Iraq War, communicated with an Iraqi general, who said that the incursion had been a mistake, that Iraq had no intention of invading the Kingdom, and that Iraqi troops would be instructed to stay strictly on the Kuwaiti side of the border. Some Saudis believed that the assurances were intended to lull Saudi Arabia into believing that it was not in danger; others believed that Iraq did not have territorial ambitions, the *New York Times* reported.

But six hours later, there was a second incursion. Once again the Saudis called the Iraqi command post on the hotline telephone. The Iraqi general who had provided the assurances was not available, the Saudis were told. His absence heightened Saudi suspicions that the previous assurances were a smokescreen for a planned invasion. A more junior officer came to the hotline and said that he knew nothing of the border incursion but would check with his superiors and call back with an explanation. No one called back.

Six hours later, there was a third incursion. A Saudi officer tried the hot line for the third time in less than twenty-four hours. This time there was no reply.[11]

After his meeting at the Pentagon, Bandar called King Fahd to tell him the satellite photos confirmed that the threat to Saudi Arabia was real. After King Fahd confirmed that Prince Bandar had seen the photos with his own eyes, he agreed to accept an American delegation that would bring the latest U.S. intelligence, including updated satellite photos.

The next day's satellite shots revealed seven ground-to-ground Scud missile launchers outside Kuwait City, amied south at Saudi Arabia. That afternoon, August 5, Cheney departed in a jet from the United States, leading the American delegation that would meet with King Fahd the following day.

As the U.S. delegation took the overnight flight to Jeddah, King Fahd carried on intense discussions within the royal family. Because he is a king, many westerners believe that he can simply hand down orders quickly and arbitrarily whenever he wants something done. The fact that King Fahd seldom fulfills this Western stereotypical image of a king leads many to believe that he is slow and indecisive. What most westerners don't understand however, are the traditional customs and mores of the Saudi's Islamic system of government. Saudi leaders, and King Fahd in particular, believe strongly in the importance of considering and debating various viewpoints, reaching the correct decision through this process and then building a consensus around the decision. Because this debate generally is carried out within the closed circle of the ruling family, most westerners simply do not realize that it exists.

But debate was raging that night, and for good

reason. For years, the Saudis had rejected American requests to base its troops in the Kingdom. In fact, during the Iran-Iraq War, the United States had surprised the Saudis with CIA intelligence reports alleging that Iran was coming across the narrow Persian Gulf to attack them. The Reagan Administraton had formally requested permission to deploy U.S. Air Force fighters to stop these expected attacks. The Saudis had refused. The attacks never materialized, and the Saudis concluded that the United Stated used intelligence for its goal of stationing its troops in Saudi soil.

On the other hand, the Kuwaitis were so blind to Iraq's military threat and so suspicious of American intentions that it failed to seek the help it needed in time.

Aside from security concerns, a major factor not readily understood by westerners was relifion, and the protection of Makkah and Madinah, the two holiest sites in the Islamic world. In fact, King Fahd's official title if "Custodian of the Holy Places of Mecca and Medina." Islamic law prohibits non-Muslims from being near the holy sites. In reality, the holy sites, located near the Red Sea, were far removed from the Eastern Province and the Kuwaiti border. There was little danger of the sites being overrun by Iraqi troops or need for non-Islamic troops to be anywhere near them.

After the sixteen hour flight, Cheney arrived at the King's private council room with General Norman Schwartzkopf, CIA Deputy Robert Gates, Paul Wolfowitz, Undersecretary of State for Policy, Pete Williams, a DOD press officer and U.S. Ambassador to Saudi Arabia, Charles W. Freeman, Jr. They were greeted by the King, Crown Prince Abdullah, Prince Bandar, and six government officials, including the Foreign Minister and the Deputy Defense Minister.

Dispensing with the usual formalities, King Fahd politely directed Cheney to get right to the point.

Cheney opened the briefing by explaining the United States' two-part plan of defending Saudi Arabia and applying economic pressure to Iraq. Then General Schwartzkopf brought out the latest satellite photos showing Iraqi tank movements toward the Saudi border, well secured resupply lines, repositioned attach aircraft and Scud missile launchers pointing south.[12]

The briefing helped the Saudis resolve one question. Previously, they had sent scouts to the border and found no sign of Iraqi troops or tanks. But the photos showed the Iraqis moved their command, control, and communications units ahead of the armored divisions, and were too small to spot easily.

Schwartzkopf said Iraq was in position to attack Saudi Arabia within forty-eight hours, but he quickly conceded that he did not know what Saddam's true intentions were.

Having seen what he was waiting for, King Fahd finally spoke, stating that he did not see any ambiguity. "They have forces in position that are not needed just for Kuwait," he said of the Iraqi army. "Therefore they must have other objectives."

King Fahd said the key issue was trust and credibility, stating that Saudi rulers used to think Saddam Hussein told the truth. The King cited Saddam's promise to himself, the United States and to Mubarak that he wouldn not attack Kuwait, but the opposite happened. So we know his bad intentions are there, the King said.

Schwartzkopf went on to describe the huge force the United States could mobilize -- up to 250,000 troops, Air Force planes, and Navy ships.

Anticipating Saudi sensitivity about foreign forces,

Cheney said, that the President asked him to assure the King that the U.S. would stay as long as the Saudis want. It would leave when no longer needed and it "will stay until justice is done but not stay a minute longer." Cheney said the U.S. was not seeking bases but that Saudi Arabia was a long way away. "We need to make joint preparations now," Cheney added.

King Fahd clearly believed the threat from Iraq was real, that the plan presented by Cheney and Schwartzkopf was a good one, that there was a firm agreement there would be no permanent positioning of foreign forces in Saudi Arabia and that U.S. equipment could be left in position in case of future emergencies. The two sides subsequently agreed that if American troops had to be stationed in the region, they could be placed in Bahrain or in liberated Kuwait.[13]

Indicating his desire to go forward, King Fahd set the framework for unprecedented strategic cooperation, telling the U.S. delegation that the basis for Saudi cooperation with the United States was the threat to Saudi Arabia and mutual interests. The goal was not to attack others or to be aggressors.

He pointed out that Saddam had created the problem in part by spending so much money on armaments, instead of things for his people. He said Saddam was egotistical, was aspiring to something larger than just Kuwait, but that he had made a big mistake.

In keeping with Saudi custom, the King asked his delegation for comments. This prompted a lively debate in Arabic which only the U.S. Ambassador, who spoke Arabic, could understand.

King Fahd concluded, "We have to do this. The Kuwaitis waited, they waited too long and now there no longer is a Kuwait."

Prince Bandar, translating the session, announced

the agreement in principle, and suggested that the military people proceed with the details.

King Fahd demonstrated to the U.S. delegation that when important decisions had to be made, he could do so quickly. After Cheney thanked him, the King said that they did not have the luxury of time. They faced immediate dangers. What needed to be done quickly must be done at once, he said.

As the meeting adjourned, he expressed approval of a U.S. military team staying in Saudi Arabi, adding, "The quicker the work gets done, the better."[14]

King Fahd explained to the U.S. delegation that joint development projects with various western nations had proven key to Saudi Arabia's incredible conversion from a backward desert country to one with a modern infrastructure, seven universities, and 37 junior colleges.

He said the Saudi people's belief in Islam gives them both confidence and humility, so that they are willing to learn from other peoples, and are not bothered by unfounded criticism.

He said he scoffed at a report that the Saudi royal family had an income of $40 billion a year, stating that the sum was greater than the whole country's gross national product.

"Many preposterous things are said, but I don't care what is said outside. What I care about is the welfare and well-being of the Saudi people."

In closing, King Fahd sent thanks to President Bush and the Congress, expressing gratitude that the sole objective was to help Saudi Arabia.[15]

At the same time the Saudis and Americans met in Jeddah, and while Iraqi armored divisions established positions at the Saudi border, Saddam Hussein met with Joseph Wilson, the American charge d'affaires in Baghdad. Saddam downplayed the significance of the invasion, and said he "did not understand" the United States' concern over "Iraq's intentions with respect to Saudi Arabia." Saddam said Iraq had signed a non-aggression pact with Saudi Arabia.[16]

"If you are really worried about Saudi Arabia, your worries are unfounded, but if you are showing that worry in order to worry Saudi Arabia, that is something else. We will say the same thing to our Saudi brothers, and we are ready to give them any guarantees that they want, to remove that worry. More than that, if there is a foreign danger, we feel that it is our duty to protect Saudi Arabia," Saddam told Wilson.[17]

In direct response to a question by Wilson, Saddam Hussein offered assurances that he would not undertake military action against Saudi Arabia.

He said he was not "annoyed" that King Fahd received the Emir of Kuwait, but warned, "We will only be annoyed if they allow them to work against Iraq from Saudi Arabia."

It seemed a classic Saddam ploy that was becoming all too familiar to those watching closely. First, he offered assurances of peaceful intentions, but makes them contingent upon a vague condition -- this time that the Kuwaiti government not be allowed to "work against" Iraq after it invaded and captured their country. Presumably, Saddam's statement meant that any Kuwaiti government official who spoke out against the Iraqi invasion from Saudi soil would provide justification for an Iraqi move against Saudi Arabia.

Saddam also told Wilson: "By the way, say hello to President Bush and tell him to consider the Jaber family, and the group that is with them, finished, history. The family of Sabah is history."[18]

President Bush, who personally promised the Emir of Kuwait that he would be restored to power, probably found very little reassuring in Saddam's statements about Saudi Arabia, and most likely took as taunting his final comment about the Emir.

On August 8, President Bush addressed the nation, announcing that he had, at the request of the Saudi government, sent troops to Saudi Arabia to assist in the defense of the Kingdom.

"In the life of a nation, we're called upon to define who we are and what we believe. Sometimes the choices are not easy. I ask for your support in the decision I have made to stand up for what's right and condemn what's wrong all in the cause of peace."

Bush called for the immediate unconditional and complete withdrawal of all Iraqi forces, and announced the economic embargo against Iraq and the freezing of its assets.

"Let me be clear, the sovereign independence of Saudi Arabia is of vital interest to the United States. This decision, which I shared with the congressional leadership, grows out of the long-standing friendship and security relationship between the United States and Saudi Arabia. U.S. forces will work together with those of Saudi Arabia and other nations to preserve the integrity of Saudi Arabia and to deter further Iraqi aggression. Through their presence, as well as through training and exercises, these multinational forces will enhance the overall capability of Saudi armed forces to defend the Kindgom."[19]

Immediately after Bush's broadcast, the Revolution Command Council in Baghdad issued a communique announcing the "annexation of Kuwait." The move was described as a "permanent union."

The next day Saddam Hussein received Yasser Arafat and Abu Iyad, two PLO leaders that were making a last-ditch effort for a diplomatic solution.[20]

Saddam said he would not go to the Arab Summit if the Emir of Kuwait was there. He only agreed to explore a peace plan if the PLO could convince King Fahd, President Mubarak, King Hussein, and President Assad to come to Baghdad -- a long shot at best.

Saddam was more intent on talking of his war plans, stating that if attacked by the United States, he would attack Israel. This would portray the conflict as Arab against American-Zionist, and dissuade Egypt and Syria from supporting the coalition. Second, he explained, the Iraqi army was strengthening its circular lines of defense of Kuwait City, which would require U.S. ground forces to suffer enormous casualties -- even with air superiority.

The third aspect of his plan concerned Saudi Arabia. It was a plan that contradicted most of the assurances he had offered earlier and confirmed King Fahd's worst suspicions.

Saddam told Arafat, "A group has been formed composed of Iraqis and Saudis, ready to launch terrorist attacks against American troops stationed on Saudi territory. If war breaks out, there will be fighting within Saudi Arabia. In the past five years dozens of arms, mostly of Polish or Czech manufacture, have been smuggled across the border from Yemen. They are now in the hands of tribesmen hostile to the Saudi royal family."[21]

No one will ever know what would have happened had the King not accepted foreign military assistance. It is possible that the Iraqi army would have stayed in Kuwait. But Saddam's statement to Arafat, combined with contingency plans for takeover of the United Arab Emirates taken from captured Iraqi paratroopers, indicated that Saddam was willing to go as far as the world would allow to achieve his dream of becoming a first-rate world power.

1. Based on interviews with confidential sources.
2. Ibid.
3. *Secret Dossier,* pg. 85.
4. Ibid., pg. 104.
5. Ibid., pg. 98.
6. Confidential sources.
7. *New York Times,* Aug. 5, 1990, pg. 12.
8. *The Commanders,* pg. 240.
9. Ibid., pg. 240.
10. *The Commanders,* pg. 243.
11. *New York Times,* Oct. 4, 1990.
12. Ibid., pg. 268.
13. *Secret Dossier,* pg. 136.
14. Memorandum of conversation written by U.S. Ambassador to Saudi Arabia, Charles Freeman III.
15. Ibid., to memo of conversation.
16. *Secret Dossier,* pgs. 138-39.
17. Ibid.
18. Ibid., pg. 144.
19. Bush speech, August 8, 1990.
20. *Secret Dossier,* pg. 155.
21. *Secret Dossier,* pg. 159.

5

GULF WAR DIPLOMACY: A GAP NEVER BRIDGED

The invasion of Kuwait set many things in motion. Internally, it forced Saudi Arabia, the United States, and major countries of western Europe to prepare for war.

The invasion also touched off what perhaps turned out to be the most extensive campaign of international diplomacy ever by members of the United Nations and prominent private citizens groping for a formula to avoid war.

The period was one of great transition for low-key Saudi leaders, who were known for preferring a behind-the-scenes role when it came to regional and international matters. But the invasion, the subsequent military buildup, and search for a peaceful settlement had thrust the Saudis onto center stage.

Because of King Fahd's willingness to let King Hussein's initial diplomatic efforts run their course, there was no official Saudi communication about the invasion for several days. For instance, August 3, the day following the invasion, the headline in the English-speaking *Arab News* read, "King Fahd Strives To Ease Tension." Most Arabic language Saudi newspapers did not fully report the invasion until several days after it occurred.

Once the King had met with the U.S. delegation and

decided that he could not afford to trust Saddam Hussein, he quickly moved to explain the events leading to Iraq's invasion, and his reasons for accepting the assistance of foreign militaries in defense of the Kingdom.

In an August 9 televised address, he said, "You undoubtedly know that the government of the Kingdom of Saudi Arabia has exerted all possible efforts with the governments of the Iraqi Republic and the State of Kuwait to contain the dispute between the two countries."

"In this context, I made numerous telephone calls and held fraternal talks with the brothers. As a result, a bilateral meeting was held between the Iraq and Kuwait delegations in Saudi Arabia with the aim of bridging the gap and narrowing the differences to avert any further escalation."

"However, regrettably enough, events took an adverse course to our endeavors . . . resulting in an invasion that inflicted painful suffering on the Kuwaitis and rendered them homeless," he said, calling the invasion "the most horrible act of aggression that the Arab nation has known in its modern history."

King Fahd called for the restoration of the Kuwaiti government and the return of its territory. He said that U.S., British, and other Arab troops accepted his invitation to assist in the defense of his nation, adding that their status was "temporary."

"They will leave Saudi territory immediately at the request of the Kingdom," he said.

Three days later, King Fahd explained to an audience of Saudis that he was committed simultaneously to the principles of non-aggression and defense.

"We are a country that does not like to initiate aggression against anyone. But we would all rather die than allow anyone to launch an aggression against a single inch of our territory. If such aggression takes place, we will wage jihad (holy war) to defend our land, dignity, and honor."

The Iraqi troops amassing on the border posed a threat to all Saudis' freedom, particularly the freedom to worship.

"I would like to assure [Saudi] citizens that I will allow neither myself nor anyone else to interfere in the public or private affairs of citizens, including the freedom that has been guaranteed them by Islam. . . . (We) will do our utmost to protect them and their Islamic faith."

"Arab and Islamic traditions require that a person stand by his words and promises. What causes much pain is that the invasion was conducted by a strong country against one with limited capabilities. . . . [Kuwait] was taken by surprise because of the Iraqi assurance that it would not use force," he said.

"How can we believe that Saddam Hussein does not plan aggression against the Kingdom of Saudi Arabia? He already has reneged on his promises and has invaded Kuwait despite the guarantees and promises he made to me and to President Hosni Mubarak of Egypt," King Fahd said.

On August 11, Saudi Arabia and Egypt persuaded a majority of Arab League members to condemn the invasion, demand the restoration of the Kuwaiti government, and vote in favor of sending troops to defend Saudi Arabia. Saddam Hussein, reflecting the importance of Islam to political debate in the Middle East, called on "Arabs and Muslims, faithful everywhere to rise and defend Makkah, which is captured by the spears of the Americans and Zionists. . . . Keep the foreigner away from your holy shrines." The words may have rung hollow to those who realized that Saddam was an atheist. But they appealed to anti-western sentiments among the masses in poorer Arab nations.

In a statement issued by August 13, the Saudi government reminded Iraq that Saudi Arabia was instrumental in building up the Iraqi army so it could defend itself against Iran, and serve as a shield in the service of the Palestinian cause, "and a liberator of Jerusalem from the desecration of Zionist occupation. The Iraqi leadership uses that army against the Arab nation in its aggression against Kuwait and it threatens to use it against other Arab countries."

Challenging Saddam's religious references, it said, "Those who are now calling for a 'holy war' are the farthest from the teachings of Islam and its tenets than anyone else. Could anyone consider the acts of the Iraqi leadership in shedding blood, plundering properties and raping women in Kuwait permissible by Islam?"

King Fahd also was clear on the Saudis' intent of establishing its defenses in the face of large Iraqi forces.

Vowing that no first strike would be launched from Saudi soil in the opening phase of Desert Shield, King Fahd said, "The Kingdom will not start any aggression unless it is subjected to an attack and I am committed to this. But we have no control over any shots fired from outside the Kingdom."

Asked about the possibility of a simultaneous withdrawal of the Iraqi forces from Kuwait and of the foreign forces from the Gulf, the King said, "We first of all have to know if Iraq is ready to withdraw. We don't want to attack anyone and I will stand by this unless we ourselves are attacked."[1]

The Saudi people responded favorably to the call for action. On August 20, King Fahd began the process of strengthening the armed forces by ordering the opening of recruitment and training centers around the country. He also announced that various government ministries were monitoring economic developments closely, and offered assurances that the market would remain stable.[2] On August 27, he ordered the opening of a special counter at the recruitment centers for receiving applications of citizens who wanted to join regular military service and another one for receiving applications from volunteers.[3]

The United Nations moved quickly to enforce an economic blockade against Iraq. On August 18, the UN Security Council warned Iraq of possible military action unless it immediately freed all foreigners being held hostages. The following day, Saddam announced that he would free 10,000 foreigners if President Bush pledged complete U.S. military and political withdrawal from the Persian Gulf. On August 21, the Iraqi leader floated peace proposals with King Hussein, but Bush rejected them because they did not begin with the withdrawal of Iraqi forces from Kuwait. The war of words steadily escalated between Bush and Saddam Hussein.[4] Soviet Union President Mikhail Gorbachev also warned Saddam to withdraw from Kuwait, signaling that the USSR would support a UN resolution authorizing military steps to enforce an embargo against Iraq.[5]

In what set off a virtual parade to Baghdad, President Kurt Waldheim of Austria and Rev. Jesse Jackson announced they would fly to Iraq to meet with Saddam about releasing hostages and the prospects for peace.

One of the most important figures to travel to Baghdad was UN Secretary General Javier Perez de Cuellar. But after two long days of meetings with Iraqi Foreign Minister Tariq Aziz, de Cuellar announced that he had failed to produce any concessions from Baghdad on its occupation of Kuwait or on its policy of holding an estimated 10,000 westerners as hostages.[6]

Possibly because they knew Saddam better than anyone else in the region, the Saudis appeared to lose hope very early that diplomatic efforts would persuade Saddam to withdraw the army from Kuwait. They focused many of their efforts on preparing for war both at home and in the international community. The Saudis' new-found activism was reflected in the resignation of Chedli Kilibi, who had been Secretary General of the Arab League for ten years. The Saudi and Syrian Foreign Ministers complained that Klibi did not do enough to persuade more Arab states to send troops to Saudi Arabia to guard against possible Iraqi attack. At that point, only Syria, Egypt and Morocco had sent troops.[7]

On September 4, King Fahd issued a sweeping directive to mobilize Saudi society for possible war with Iraq. The directive mandated an expansion of the armed forces, which traditionally had been carefully selected in order to strike a geographic and tribal balance, by opening the way for all male university graduates to enroll immediately in any branch of service. He also ordered all specialized government authorities to accept women volunteers.[8]

On September 6, the Saudi government announced that it would cover virtually all of the hundreds of millions of dollars in monthly operating costs of the American forces based in and near Saudi Arabia.[9]

The same day, Soviet President Mikhail Gorbachev refused to offer Iraq any solace. In a meeting with Iraqi Foreign Minister Tariq Aziz, Gorbachev called Iraq's invasion unprovoked and reiterated the Soviet Government's demand for an immediate withdrawal.[10] The previous day, Soviet Foreign Minister Eduard

Shevardnadze proposed convening an international conference on the Mideast as a means of resolving the crisis. But the proposal was not considered seriously by those nations demanding complete withdrawal.

Gorbachev met with Bush September 9 in Helsinki, Finland. The two issued a joint pledge to act "individually and in concert" to reverse Iraq's conquest of Kuwait, even if peaceful means failed.

Tariq Aziz then went to Tehran. Although Iranian Foreign Minister Ali Akbar Velayati criticized the buildup of western forces in the Gulf, he publicly condemned Iraq's invasion of Kuwait.[11]

One week later, French President Francois Mitterand ordered 4,000 soldiers and dozens of planes, helicopters, and tanks to Saudi Arabia in response to Iraq's moves against French diplomats in Kuwait. This represented another blow to Iraq, as it traditionally enjoyed closer ties to France than any other western nation.[12]

On September 20, the Bush Administration rejected a peace proposal by King Hussein that would have involved simultaneous withdrawal of non-Arab forces from the Gulf and Iraqi forces from Kuwait. Unnamed Administration officials told the *New York Times* that it objected to the proposal because by linking the two withdrawals it established an unspecified "privileged relationship" between Iraq and Kuwait in the future. The officials also objected to lumping together Gulf problems and the issues of the occupied West Bank and Lebanon.

The incident prompted Prince Hassan, King Hussein's brother, to complain that the United States consistently had undercut Jordanian peace efforts.

"Every time a group of leaders say they have a package, the first thing that happens is that the

Americans knock it down by beginning with the assumption that nothing short of complete Iraqi withdrawal is acceptable," the Prince said.

He added, "To be symmetrical, the Iraqis have not been too forthcoming either."

He said that the Americans should realize that "the problem with the Iraqis is that every time something happens to pressure them, they become more adamant on the question of withdrawal."

Still, King Hussein continued shuttling between Rabat, Morocco and Algeria and Baghdad in search of a peace proposal. A Jordanian official said there was a chance that King Fahd would join King Hussein for a meeting with the Iraqi President in Baghdad, but Saudi officials dismissed the idea.[13]

Saddam Hussein, realizing that he may have been mistaken to think that the seizure of Kuwait would improve his negotiating position, began to show his frustration. On September 23, he lashed out, asserting that he would order a preemptive attack on the Saudi oil fields, other Arab members of the coalition, and Israel.

"The oil areas in Saudi Arabia and in other states of the region, all the oil installations, will be rendered incapable of responding to the needs of those who came to us as occupiers in order to usurp our sovereignty, dignity, and wealth," he said.[14]

Relations between Jordan and Saudi Arabia continued to decline. On September 25, the Saudis expelled twelve more Jordanian diplomats accusing them of spying for Iraq.[15] Later, it was discovered that the Palestine Liberation Organization helped meet the payroll of Iraqi diplomats in various nations where Iraqi banks accounts had been depleted.

Also on September 25, Shevardnadze, seeking to remove any doubt about the Soviet position, told the UN

General Assembly September 25, that war would be imminent if Iraq failed to pull out of Kuwait.

On October 2, Saudi Minister of Foreign Affairs Prince Saud Al-Faisal addressed the United Nations General Assembly. The occasion was the election of the new UN President. It served as a platform for Prince Saud to outline his country's position on the Gulf crisis.

He explained how King Fahd attempted to avoid the crisis by organizing the Jeddah meeting, and how Saudi Arabia was taken by surprise by Iraq's sudden attack. He reiterated that the invasion violated all international laws and treaties, including the Charters of the League of Arab States and the United Nations. He repeated the call for Iraq's unconditional withdrawal from Kuwait and restoration of its government.

"We do not break promises and accept no threats. Thus our leadership has taken the firm decisions that will ensure the protection of land and man, the protection of vital economic assets, and the consolidation of defensive capabilities," Prince Saud said, explaining that the Saudi Arabia's acceptance of foreign troops was in keeping with Article 51 of the UN Charter as well as the Charter of the Arab League. He reminded the General Assembly that the foreign forces' stay in the Kingdom was temporary.

"Our leadership has carried out their responsibilities and accounted for the anticipated development of events so that the Kuwaiti catastrophe would not recur and that it will not be taken by the surprise of adventures."

Prince Saud charged that Iraq's actions were an affront to the Arab world and to Islam. "We, in the Kingdom of Saudi Arabia, wonder: How an Arab solution can be reached on the ruins of another Arab state? How to reach solutions when the government of Iraq has blocked all the roads? And how to join in the international march towards new international cooperation if we forgive the usurpation by an Arab of an Arab land?"

"God honored us by carrying the message of Islam, we raised with humility and pride the banner of justice, helping the oppressed and rescuing the anxious. We stand above violating the rights of the neighbor and the sanctity of the brother, and pillaging for spoils. These are genuine morals, and our magnanimous Islamic principles which define us. It is not acceptable or reasonable to apply to our behavior and actions as Arabs lower standards and formulae that those that other nations adhere to. . . . This nation must be an example in adhering to civilized and moral behavior emanating from its high ideals and principles."

Most offensive, he continued, was Iraq's claim that the invasion of Kuwait would advance the Palestinians' quest for their homeland. "It pains us that attention is being diverted from the Intifadah of the heroic Palestinian people, the steps to search for a just solution are retreating, and the dangers of Jewish immigration to the occupied territories are passing without outcry or protest. It pains us more that the Iraqi regime, which claims a monopoly over the salvation of Palestine, is following the same Israeli method of occupying the land, dispersing the people, and refusing withdrawal. Rather, it offers Israel an international justification to consecrate occupation and to empty the homeland from its people and replace them with immigrants. Thus, it is for Palestine that Iraq should withdraw from Kuwait and adhere to international legitimacy so that we can mobilize international legality to realize for the people of Palestine what will be realized for the people of Kuwait."

The Iraqi response was given at the UN October 5

by Foreign Deputy Minister Sabah Talat Kadrat, who said Iraq would not withdraw from Kuwait and accused the United States of "Western Imperialism."

In the following weeks, several prominent officials travelled to Baghdad to seek release of foreigners being held in Iraq and to convince Saddam that withdrawal is the only course that will avoid war. These included former British Prime Minister Edward Heath, boxing great Muhammad Ali, former U.S. Attorney General Ramsey Clark, and former Japanese Prime Minister Nakasone.

Moreover, former Nicaraguan President Daniel Ortega spent most of November working on a "non-aligned movement" plan to bring peace, that was supported by Willy Brandt, former West German Chancellor, and Rajiv Ghandhi, former Prime Minister of India.

While these efforts may have contributed to the release of foreign hostages, they failed to move the situation any closer to a diplomatic resolution.

At one point, observers detected a possible softening in the Saudi stance when Saudi Defense Minister Prince Sultan told journalists, "Saudi Arabia has said, and says now, that giving rights, including territorial brotherly concessions - given willingly - is a matter of pride for the Arab nations."

While some thought this meant that the Saudis would go along with a proposal that would grant Iraq some Kuwaiti land in exchange for a withdrawal, Prince Sultan said his remarks had been misinterpreted.

To emphasize the point, King Fahd issued a statement that Saudi demands for Iraqi withdrawal "are not subject to bargaining or misinterpretations" and that "any understanding or predictions that fall outside those clear parameters" emanating from any individuals "or are yet to be uttered in the future are untrue and should be paid no attention at all."

King Fahd's remarks, which were termed by one official as a "countdown to war," reportedly "caused Saudis as well as foreign diplomats in Riyadh to speculate on when, not if, war with Iraq would begin."[16]

Ten days later, the United States and Saudi Arabia agreed that any offensive against Iraqi troops begun from Saudi territory would be undertaken only after President Bush and King Fahd both gave their approval. Moreover, the accord gave American commanders the authority necessary to carry out battle plans as they saw fit.[17]

Of course, the official countdown to war began November 29 when the United Nations Security Council voted 12 to 2 with 1 abstention to authorize the United States and its allies to expel Iraq from Kuwait by force if Saddam Hussein failed to withdraw by January 15.

The Security Council vote set off another frenzied round of diplomatic efforts. They began immediately when Bush invited Iraqi Foreign Minister Tariq Aziz to visit Washington, and offered to send Secretary of State James Baker to meet with President Hussein in Baghdad. Bush was in part responding to public opinion surveys showing that Americans feared their President was not working hard enough on diplomatic solutions. But Bush's sudden announcement annoyed many of his Arab coalition partners, who knew that Saddam Hussein would take it as a sign of weakness.

The Saudis, for instance, continued to express little interest in bargaining. Algerian President Chadli Benjedid met with Saddam Hussein in Baghdad, hoping to come up with a peace proposal. But the Saudis advised Benjedid that a visit to Riyadh would serve no useful purpose unless the Iraqi President accepted the principle of total and unconditional withdrawal from Kuwait.[18]   As weeks passed, and it became apparent that Saddam Hussein had no intention of withdrawing the Iraqi army from Kuwait, King Fahd aired a series of clear warnings that the coalition forces were prepared to use force to achieve Iraq's withdrawal.

The first came November 28, 1990, on the eve the United Nations vote to authorize military action against Iraq. Meeting with Saudi newspaper editors, King Fahd bluntly warned Saddam that if he did not withdraw from Kuwait, "it will be a tragedy for Iraq."[19]

Citing the futility of negotiations, King Fahd asked the editors, "Negotiations on what? To compensate the aggressor? I don't think anyone will even consider it."

It was noteworthy that on this occasion King Fahd reemphasized the sense of betrayal he felt against Saddam Hussein, stating that Saddam promised him personally on August 1 that he would not invade Kuwait, only to invade the next day and send an envoy the day after that to tell the King privately that he had annexed Kuwait once and for all.

"We never thought of an Arab state invading another Arab state," King Fahd said. "Then I realized that after Kuwait, it would be the turn of the eastern part of the Kingdom."

On December 3. Prince Khalid bin Sultan, a Saudi lieutenant general and commander of the Arab forces, underlined the readiness and willingness of the Saudi army to fight.

"We believe that if our [U.S.] friends are here to shed their blood for us, the least we can do is to put [our] forces right in the front," he said. "And if there is any bloodshed, I can assure you, Saudis will take it before their friends."[20]

Acknowledging   that   the   Saudi   army   was

incxperienced, Prince Khalid said, "If anybody touches my land or there is any order by his majesty [King Fahd], you will see vicious soldiers who will do their job well. That I can promise."

During this period the *Washington Post* reported a major divergence in prediction by American and Saudi military officials.

"The Americans, perhaps planning for the worst, think the Iraqis will be difficult foes. Saudis say they don't think the Iraqis will put up much of a fight," the *Post* reported.

"I'm sure of that," one Saudi officer told the *Post*, citing the Iraqi army's low morale and poor supply lines. He said the Saudi army already had received at least 300 defectors from Iraqi lines inside Kuwait.[21]

"Asked to explain this difference in American and Saudi expectations of the Iraqis' war-time performance, another Saudi replied: 'We know [the Iraqis] better' than the Americans," the *Post* reported.

One month later, after inspecting front-line troops, King Fahd was conciliatory, stating that he was still hopeful of a peaceful solution and calling on Saddam Hussein to come to his senses. "I hope that President Saddam will take this bold step to spare the region a catastrophic war," he said at the Hafr al-Baten air force base near the Kuwaiti border.[22] The same day, however, Saddam, in a televised address, said his army was ready for a long war, making his famous comment that "the mother of all battles will also be waged under an experienced, cohesive military leadership. It would be an honor for the believers to fight in one of the days of this battle."

In its last-ditch effort, the European Community promised to work to resolve all Mideast problems if the Persian Gulf crisis could be settled peacefully, but said the main problem was Iraq's refusal to pull out of Kuwait.[23]

However, on January 9, Aziz and Baker emerged from a six-hour meeting in Geneva and announced they had made no progress toward resolving the conflict. Both Bush and Hussein said they were ready for war.

Only three days before the January 15 UN deadline, King Fahd for the last time appealed to Saddam Hussein's sense of reason.

"We don't want to see Iraq and its people destroyed, but if President Saddam continues his adamant stand, he will be responsible for the consequences. . . and then [war] will be lawful," King Fahd said in address at a gathering of Muslim scholars, the *Ulema*, at Makkah. The choice of Makkah as the site of his final appeal to Saddam, and the *Ulema* as the audience, was seen as a powerful one, as it reminded Saddam that the Islamic world predominantly had condemned the Iraqi invasion of Kuwait and supported the use of force to reverse it.

King Fahd emphasized that the border disputes between Iraq and Kuwait could be resolved peacefully, at "Arab, Islamic, or international levels."

He referred to Saddam Hussein's surprise decision to withdraw his troops from Iran, adding, "It will not be difficult for President Saddam to do the same for Kuwait."

He reminded Saddam his adamancy will cause incalculable losses to the Iraqi people and pointed out the sufferings of the Iraqis due to the UN embargo. He said Saddam had made a serious mistake, but said there was still time for him to return to "truth and reason," and accept the will of the international community.

"The door of repentance is open," he said.

The final straw came January 14 when de Cuellar went to Baghdad, but failed to convince Saddam to withdraw his forces from Kuwait.

On January 16, after picking up an Iraqi radio broadcast in which Saddam Hussein said that Saudi Arabia only extended some 11.5 million in dinars in assistance to Iraq as a result of its war with Iran, King Fahd published an open reply wich listed, in detail, the $25 billion in aid Saudi Arabia gave to Iraq.

The message concluded:

"In unanimity, the entire world through the Arab, Islamic and international resolutions called for your immediate and unconditional withdrawal from Kuwait and the restoration of legitimacy to Kuwait as well as the withdrawal of your troops massed along the Kingdom's borders. Mediators from different countries have exerted intensive efforts to convince you to remove injustice and restore the situation that prevailed before August 2, 1990, but you have rejected and insisted on continuing aggression, claiming that Kuwait was part of Iraq. God knows that Kuwait was never under Iraqi rule and the members of the family of Al-Sabah have been rulers of Kuwait for 250 years.[24]

The air war began several hours after the King's reply was broadcast.

---

1. *Arab News,* Sunday, August 12, 1990, pg. 1.
2. *Arab News,* August, 21, 1990. pg. 1.
3. *Arab News,* August 29, 1990.
4. *New York Times,* August 22, 1990.
5. *New York Times,* August 25, 1990.
6. *New York Times,* Sept. 3, 1990, pg. 1.
7. *New York Times,* Sept. 4, 1990, pg. 8.
8. *New York Times,* Sept. 5, 1990.
9. *New York Times,* Sept. 7, 1992.
10. *Tass,* Sept. 7, 1990.

11. *New York Times,* Sept. 10, 1990.
12. *New York Times,* Sept. 16, 1990.
13. *New York Times,* Sept. 21, 1990.
14. Associated Press, Sept. 23, 1990.
15. *New York Times,* Sept. 26, 1990.
16. *New York Times,* Oct. 27, 1990, pg. 4.
17. *New York Times,* Nov. 6, 1990, pg. 1.
18. *New York Times,* Dec. 14, 1990, pg. 14.
19. *New York Times,* Nov. 29, 1990.
20. *Washington Post,* Dec. 4, 1990.
21. Ibid.
22. *Arab News,* Jan. 7, 1991.
23. *New York Times,* Jan. 5, 1991.
24. *Arab News,* Jan. 17, 1991.

6

FROM SHIELD TO STORM: HOSTING THE BUILDUP

As we have seen, the events leading up to the invasion of Kuwait posed a series of difficult and momentous decisions for leaders around the world, as debates raged in most countries over the appropriate response to Saddam Hussein.

However, making a decision is one thing; implementing it is quite another. King Fahd, President Bush, and other western and Arab world leaders were resolute about first stopping the Iraqi army and, ultimately, reversing the seizure of Kuwait. But the major question was whether they were up to the task? Saddam Hussein appeared to have based his moves on the opinion that the Gulf states in the West would never stand up to him, or, if they did, he could defeat them on the harsh desert battlefield.

It is often said that "war is an arm of diplomacy." But at times in history, the logistics of fighting a war have had the potential for ending the battle before it begins. In 1903 in the United States, the Hearst newspapers, known for their sensationalist approach to the news, whipped up a furor over Spain's continued colonization of Cuba. Following the explosion aboard the U.S.S. Maine in Havana harbor, an incident that in all likelihood was manufactured as a "final straw," President McKinley ordered Teddy Roosevelt and the Rough Riders to drive the Spaniards out. U.S. history books tell the story of Roosevelt leading his men to a climatic victory.

What most Americans are not taught is that Roosevelt, due to logistical miscalculations of farcical proportions, almost never made it to Cuba. He had led the would-be troops to Florida so they could set sail for Havana. What nobody realized was that there were no roads connecting northern Florida to Miami. Roosevelt and company ended up hacking their way through unfriendly terrain, with many men taking sick and a few dying from malaria and other tropical maladies. (If you are wondering how the Rough Riders managed to defeat the Spaniards after this horrible trek, it was mainly because there were very few Spaniards left in Cuba by the time they got there.)

"Logistics" describes all that goes into supporting combat troops and equipment: food, water, fuel, ammunition, transportation, and storage, just to name a few. In every war, there are instances of logistical shortcomings either hampering a military's operations or dooming them altogether. In World War II, the Nazi army's lack of fuel accelerated the demise of its ground forces in the final two years of the war. In Vietnam, the U.S. Army faced many logistical problems on top of all the political problems. For instance, the country lacked adequate ports for unloading equipment, so the Army had to build them. Later, the docks were plagued by thefts and hijacking, and U.S. supplies fed a thriving black market.

From the point of military planners, the prospective fight between Iraq and the coalition forces had all the trappings of a logistical nightmare. It was inevitable that hundreds of thousands of ground troops would arrive. Just providing them with food and water in a desert environment was a challenge.

Many of the leaders of the countries which eventually made up the allied coalition, realizing that Saddam had misled them or outright lied about his intentions, quickly came to the view that it would, at a minimum, take the threat of a credible military force to restore Kuwait to its previous rulers.

The Saudi and U.S. militaries immediately went into action following the August 6 meeting between Defense Secretary Richard Cheney and King Fahd. Within six hours, the Saudis sent their some 10,000-member National Guard force to the Kuwaiti border. Of course this was not a credible deterrent, as they were up against 100,000 Iraqi troops, including two divisions of the feared Republican Guard, only some 20 and 50 miles away. But the deployment served as the first tangible signal that Saudi Arabia would not stand for any Iraqi encroachment.

The morning of August 2, U.S. Maj. General William (Gus) Pagonis briefed Lt. Gen. John Yeasock, Army Assistant Chief of Staff for Operation and Plans, prior to Yeasock's trip with the Cheney delegation to meet King Fahd. On August 5, the day before King Fahd officially invited the military in, Pagonis was ordered to join the U.S. delegation in Riyadh.

Pagonis handpicked twenty-one officers to take charge of various areas, like aerial and sea ports of debarkation, receipt of troops, equipment and supplies, sustainment, and onward movement. On August 7, Pagonis and four of his team flew in a C-130 transport to the Kingdom.

The long flight gave the Pagonis quintet a chance to

draft plans for the nuts and bolts of the military buildup, dividing it into three major tasks: receipt of personnel and their equipment in the oil-rich Saudi Eastern Province, their movement to base and staging areas, and their sustainment once they get there.

It seemed pretty simple at 30,000 feet, but by the time Pagonis reached Dharan on August 9, he could see he had his work cut out for him. Although Dharan was the heart of Aramco's Gulf coast oil installations, there was very little in the way of suitable buildings to work out of for Pagonis or his staff, or worse, adequate shelter from the 120 degree heat for the thousands of troops of the U.S. 82nd Airborne Division that began arriving at 5:00 a.m. that morning. In fact, one lieutenant colonel who arrived a day before had to spend the first night working out of the back of a station wagon with three other Americans, as the hotels were full with people whose travel plans were disrupted by the invasion, fleeing the advancing Iraqi army.

Pagonis had been around, splitting his time between the military commands in Europe, Panama, and Colorado, and the Army bureaucracy in Washington. Now he faced the challenge of his career.

Working with Saudi General Turki, Col. Mustafa and others, Pagonis set up the "Host Nation Support Cell," signalling the start of unparalleled strategic cooperation by two countries that had always held each other at arm's length. Exemplifying the "start-from-scratch" situation, the first items that Pagonis sought were buses and trucks for transporting troops and equipment.

What followed set the tone for the entire buildup that continued from that mid-August day until the war ended in late February. Like nearly all outsiders, Pagonis was not at all familiar with the Saudi system, which is based largely on personal contacts at the top. He turned to his Saudi counterparts for help. Saudi officers, with their intimate knowledge of the individuals and local families that ran truck and bus companies, connected Pagonis to the business people who had authority to make fast decisions and provide the military with what they needed.

As transportation was being lined up, the Saudi-U.S. team worked to resolve the shortage of fresh food and water that marred the arrival of the first wave of the 82nd Airborne. Within a day, 800 U.S. troops were served their first hot meal. Three hot meals a day would be served from then on.

By August 12, U.S. military personnel, working with newly arrived Saudi contractors, had off-loaded 2,434 troops, 168 vehicles, 28 helicopters and nine tanks.

A key to this good start was the U.S. military's experience in knowing what needed to be done, and the Saudis' ability to summon quickly the equipment, personnel, and materials necessary to make it happen. For instance, Army stevedores arrived without their equipment, but were able to begin unloading ships immediately because Saudi ports were adequately equipped.

The organization of truck and bus fleets was another example of the integration of U.S. and Saudi forces with Arab contractors. The fleets were broken down into units with specific duties, and U.S. military personnel was put in charge of each contractor who, in turn, directed his employees. Normally, an Army Captain would have directed such operations, but due to the enormity of the job and scarcity of personnel, sargeants ended up assuming tasking normally performed by officers.

Of course, Saudi companies rely on immigrant,

mainly Muslim, laborers from Bangladesh, Pakistan, Sri Lanka, and the Philippines. This gave the convoys a multi-ethnic makeup that remained for the course of the war.

"You're talking about two societies, which everybody said were so far apart, and here they are working as a team," Pagonis said.

He also was surprised that local troops and contractors were able to respond in a timely manner. "Traditionally in Arab culture, with simplicity of movement, execution is not done at the same pace as say, a western environment. I'm not condemning that -- they live a lot longer than we do. But in the anxiety of war, you still have exigent needs," Pagonis said.

"I could not afford to be negotiating with the wrong person. So General Sala, the Eastern Province commander, and General Turki, the base commander, allowed us to cut through a lot of red tape, because when they called somebody, I didn't get the 'number 3' or 'number 4' guy, I got the 'number 1' person of that bus or truck firm," Pagonis recalled.

"And the response of the Saudis was miraculous. You could not get U.S. firms or U.S. soldiers to respond any faster than the Saudis did. This was important because, let's face it, you go into a civilian corporation, talking to the wrong person, and you spin your wheels for days."

More generally, the military buildup benefitted from the infrastructure of ports, airstrips, and communications systems the Saudis had put in place during the construction boom of the 1980s.

"The Saudis had built magnificent facilities, ports and airports, which far exceeded what they needed for their own internal use," he continued. "They did what we always talk about in the States, (like) building an airport 200 miles away from the city. But what we do is build it twenty-five miles away, and the next thing you know you have an airport that can't expand because it is totally surrounded by homes. "

The military air fields were built in the middle of the desert and thus were expandable and able to accommodate the huge influx of C-130 transport planes, bombers, fighter jets, and other aircraft from six different nations.

The port facilities at two cities could handle all the ships the coalition could send -- up to fifteen per day -- and still continue meeting the shipping needs of the civilian population without disruption.

"The benevolency and cooperation of the Saudis is the part people don't understand. They just gave us total use of the ports and airports. They worked around their own civilian and military needs," Pagonis said.

Another benefit of the 1980s construction boom was the availability of extra transport trucks capable of moving heavy tanks and other military equipment from the Persian Gulf ports to desert staging areas some 200-300 miles away. Given the 120 degree desert heat, it was impossible to drive military vehicles these distances, as it would have increased maintenance problems and chewed up the two main roads servicing the area. By using flatbeds, the military also improved fuel efficiency for tanks and other vehicles once they started rolling.

Despite being in the oil-rich Gulf, fuel for the gas-guzzling tanks and heavy-armored equipment was very much a logistical concern in the early days of the buildup. To address the problem, Saudi Arabia immediately stepped up oil production, providing not only additional fuel for military needs but to help stabilize oil prices on the world market, which had shot up after the invasion. However, production itself was not sufficient, as the Saudis did not have a distribution system in place for the desolate desert region that was becoming the staging area. Consequently, Samarec, the Saudi oil firm, made available to the coalition command its entire fleet of 5,000 gallon tanker trucks. A third problem was the lack of special types of refined fuel, particularly jet fuel. This required Saudi Arabia to become the world's biggest importer of refined fuel.

By the end of August, three weeks after Pagonis arrived, there were 54,135 western troops in the Eastern Province, being serviced by 2,291 support personnel and a flourishing network of Saudi contractors. The basic necessities of shelter, food, water, and sanitation were in place. All western troops were briefed on the "dos and don'ts" of being "guests" under the Saudi system of Islamic law.

The successful coordination of Pagonis' 22nd Support Command with the Saudi arm and local contractors, prompted President Bush and General Schwartzkopf to make a precedent-setting move that would accelerate the buildup and enhance military readiness. Rather than following the usual plan of bringing in logistical supplies and personnel first, the United States decided to bring in its combat troops ahead of schedule and then expand the use of Gulf nation contractors for logistical support.

"It didn't make life easy," Pagonis recalled, "but we were able to accomplish it because we were able to tap into the host nation."

The numbers attest to the importance of this newfound strategy. While there were 54,135 airborne troops supported by 2,291 support personnel by the end of August 1990, a month later the number of combat personnel rose to 72,000 with support staff only rising to 2,973. In early November, the XVIII Airborne Corps was fully mobilized, with a total of 112,484 troops in place, 4,123 tracked vehicles, 31,597 wheeled vehicles, and 703 aircraft. It's important to remember that in the first months, western troops were arriving amidst uncertainty and fear that the large Iraqi army might attack or that Saddam Hussein would resort to a chemical gas attack. The efficient escalation of military presence both strengthened the coalition defensively and improved the morale of its members.

With all plans proceeding ahead of schedule, coalition leaders agreed it was time to start preparing for the offensive option aimed at removing Iraqi forces from Kuwait. On November 8, President Bush ordered the heavily mechanized VII Corps to transfer from its long-held base in Germany to the Gulf.

The arrival of the VII Corps shifted the buildup to a new phase. The main task was to set up a chain of "logistical support bases," tabbed LOGs, across the 300-mile stretch of desert between Dharan and King Khalid Military City (KKMC) near the Kuwait border.

From November to early January, some 350,000 personnel were received and moved forward, along with 9,000 aircraft, 12,400 tracked vehicles, 114,000 wheeled vehicles, 1,800 Army aircraft, including helicopters, 33,000 containers, 1.8 million short tons of cargo, and 300,000 short tons of ammunition.

When the air war started January 16, Gen. Schwartzkopf was confident that the coalition air forces had destroyed Iraq's ability to conduct surveillance of U.S. troop movements, effectively knocking out its "eyes and ears," as he would say later. He thus ordered what he called the biggest "end run" in military history, calling on the 82nd Airborne and VII Corps to move hundreds of miles west, so they would be in a position to outflank Iraqi forces and encircle them.

This was the first time in U.S. military history that two corps had to be moved simultaneously. It also kicked off the biggest truck driving marathon, as the move had to be completed within 21 days. The exercise involved 1,400 U.S. Army vehicles and 2,100 Saudi contractor trucks traveling 2,746 miles of main supply routes, for a rough total of 35 million miles in 3,568 convoys. On February 7, exactly 21 days after the sweep began, both corps were in position to launch the ground attack.

Saudi Arabia's military played an important part in the fighting. General Khalid was in charge of all Islamic troops, coordinating with Schwartzkopf, the commander of the much larger Western contingent.

The Saudi army routed the Iraqis in the first ground battle at the coastal town of Khaji. The Saudi air force was the second most active behind the United States, flying 8 percent of the sorties, including some of the more dangerous missions over Baghdad.

The vital logistical support in the Eastern Province provided by the Saudi military and contractors paralleled a larger effort by the Saudi government to underwrite aspects of the war effort. As mentioned, in what one U.S. official called a "truly heroic effort," the Saudis dramatically increased their production of oil to three million barrels per day, an amount that experts said was impossible, to compensate for the world market's loss of Kuwaiti oil, as well as Iraqi oil, due to the international embargo. After the initial steep rise in oil prices and confusion on world markets, within three months of the invasion the increase in Saudi supplies helped bring oil prices to near their pre-invasion level.

The Saudi government's main contribution was money -- an estimated $65 billion in outlays over a nine-month period. This total came to more than twice the nation's annual gross national product.

The above-described contracting for the food, water, fuel, transportation, and lodging for U.S. troops came to $16.8 billion, a bill on which the Saudis continued paying installments six months after the war ended. An estimated $4 billion was paid to support British and French troops.

While western troops arrived with their own equipment, soldiers from such countries as Senegal, Bangladesh, and Pakistan arrived with nothing. The Saudis outfitted them and provided support. Similarly, the Saudis equipped larger contingents from Egypt, Syria, Morocco, and Niger. It also paid soldiers' salaries, and those of eastern Europe and Scandinavian specialists in chemical war fare.

At home, the Saudis spent billions to accommodate 300,000 Kuwaiti refugees and 100,000 additional non-Kuwaiti, placing them in vacant high-rise apartments and, in most cases, furnishing them within two weeks.

It provided targeted assistance to members of the Islamic coalition. It provided $1.2 billion worth of free oil to Turkey to compensate for its loss of revenues when it obeyed the international embargo and shut down the pipeline carrying Iraqi oil. It gave "economic stabilization assistance" to Egypt and Syria to make up for lost income of citizens who were living in Kuwait and displaced by the Iraqi invasion.

On the international front, Saudi Arabia became very active, tying economic aid to diplomatic moves. It provided $1.5 billion in aid to the Soviet Union, which was said to encourage Soviet cooperation in unified moves against Iraq. Two members of the UN Security Council, Zambia and Zaire, whose votes were needed to effectuate a series of unanimous decisions against Iraq, both received special Saudi attention. Zambia secured a multi-million dollar oil deal and Zaire received similar levels of assistance.

On the politico-military front, the Saudis were in charge of communications interfacing with Iraqi troops. They produced the leaflets laying out clear instructions for Iraqi troops on the way in which they must surrender on the battlefield, a move that saved hundreds, if not thousands, of lives.

The Saudis operated "Radio Free Iraq," which for the first time broadcast anti-Saddam messages and other news into Iraq.

7

THE REACTIONS OF MUSLIM STATES TO THE GULF CRISIS

The Gulf Crisis was a serious challenge to Muslim solidarity. Muslim countries found themselves in one of the most difficult situations. Faced by the invasion of one Muslim country by another and determined not to let the Iraqi invasion go unchallenged, the majority of the Muslim countries working through the Organization of the Islamic Conference condemned the invasion and later supported the United Nations resolutions to send troops to force Iraq out of Kuwait. This series of decisions of the OIC members created a great deal of tensions among the general Muslim populations around the world. Unable to influence the decisions of their governments and fearful of American and allied intentions in the Muslim world, Muslim activist organizations became actively involved in the crisis. Their involvement exacerbated the crisis and many western analysts began to suspect Muslim acts of terror against western interests around the Muslim world. Simultaneously, many Muslims became wary of Western designs on their countries. In the particular case of the Arab world, the crisis polarized those who climbed onboard the American-led bandwagon and those who sympathized with the embattled Iraqis. Those who supported the American-led bandwagon did so because they found the protective umbrella of the Americans both useful and re-assuring. Those who rallied around the Iraqis threw their lot with these Arabs of the Euphrates and the Tigris, not because they necessarily hated the Americans, but because in their view a fellow Arab was being bullied about by an American president. This state of affairs in the Arab world was replicated in many ways in other parts of the Muslim world.

It was indeed against this background that one can now examine the reactions of the Muslim world to the Gulf Crisis and to the diplomatic and political maneuvering of the embattled countries. In this chapter we have four objectives in mind. The first objective is to examine the reactions of the Muslim states to the Crisis. This will be done by analyzing carefully and critically their policy statements made before United Nations bodies such as the General Assembly and the Security Council. Statements made at world bodies such as the Organization of the Islamic Conference, the Arab League, and the Organization of African Unity will also be scrutinized for insights and understanding of individual state policy. The second objective of this chapter is to study the reactions of the Islamic groups in the Muslim world to the crisis. Working on the assumption that these groups were dissatisfied with the existing international political system and that their opposition to the American-led United Nations force was an expression of solidarity with fellow Muslims in Iraq rather than an endorsement of the Baathist regime in Baghdad, this chapter argues that the tension in the Muslim world was largely due to the crisis of conscience within the Muslim world. Many of the Muslims opposed the Iraqi invasion of Kuwait. However, when the UN decided to take action against Iraq under the leadership of the United States of America, some of these same people rejected the idea on the grounds that they could not allow themselves to be used by the western countries in their campaign against Saddam Hussein. For this and other related reasons, this group of Muslims decided to oppose the stationing of non-Muslim troops in the Gulf, especially in the holy land of Arabia. The third objective of this chapter is to analyze the reactions of Muslim minorities in non-Muslim majority countries. Again, working on the assumption that these Muslims shared the same feelings and attitudes as their co-religionists elsewhere in Darul Islam and that the Gulf crisis was a great test of their loyalty to Islam and to their respective countries, this chapter argues that the Muslim minorities were divided between the partisans for the allied forces and the partisans for Saddam Hussein. Those who rallied around the UN flag did so because they opposed the illegal seizure of land by any state. Those who supported Saddam Hussein did so because they felt that their co-religionist was being ganged upon by a coalition of Western imperialists and their puppet states in the Muslim world. The fourth and last objective of this chapter is to draw a number of conclusions about the reactions of the Muslim World to the Gulf crisis. These conclusions are expected to serve a number of purposes. They can shed light on a number of issues that occupy the minds of many Muslims throughout the conflict; they can assist us in sorting out things relating to the conflict; they can guide us to a better understanding of the forces at work in the Middle East and in Muslim world.

A. Reactions of Muslim States to the Gulf Crisis

When the world woke up on August 2, 1990 and learned that the State of Kuwait was taken over by the army of Saddam Hussein of Iraq, there was a great deal of furor in the United Nations. Many of the leaders of the world felt that immediate action was necessary. The crisis was most deeply felt in the Arab and Muslim world for two reasons. The first was the deep sense of betrayal felt throughout the Arab world. To many Arabs, it was unbelievable that an Arab state would use military might to seize control of another. This was more so because of the existing state of hostility between Arabs and Israelis. The second point to bear in mind is that the Arab and Muslim worlds were caught by surprise by the invasion, and this with the fact that they could not pre-empt it or contain its fallout before it was too late, led many of the Muslim leaders and their people to a deep sense of agony. Opposed to the seizure of Muslim lands by fellow Muslims and determined to keep Nasserites from the western leaders and their people, Muslims expressed strong reservations about western troops stationed in Saudi Arabia.

In order to understand the nature of the Muslim World reactions to the crisis, let us group the Muslim countries geographically by region and then try to analyze the reactions of the countries within each of the identified regions of the world where Muslims live. The first area of attention is of course the Middle East; the second is the African continent; the third is South Asia; the fourth is Southeast Asia; the fifth is Soviet Central Asia. This region does not have any state that is accepted as a part of the Organization of the Islamic Conference. However, because of the sizable number of Muslims within its republics and the fear, real or imagined, that her inhabitants would throw their lot with Saddam Hussein, this region of the world occupied a great deal of attention among policy planners working on the resolution of the conflict.

The countries that were immediately involved in the

pre-war behind-the-scenes negotiations between Kuwait and Iraq were Saudi Arabia and Jordan. The Saudis, who would later become combatants in the prosecution of the war against Saddam, felt betrayed by Saddam. In the following passages we will attempt to reconstruct events through the eyes of the Saudis.

B. Reactions of the States

When we examine the reactions of the Middle Eastern Muslim peoples to the Gulf crisis we find that there were four different attitudes to the conflict. The first attitude was the pan-Arab feeling that the Iraqi leaders were giving history a helping hand by accelerating the speed of Arab unity. This was the position taken by the scattered groups of pan-Arabists who see in Saddam Hussein some resemblance of the old Nasserite image. To these Arabs, the Western countries have been patronizing the monarchs in their neighborhood and for this and other related reasons, things have never gone right. Gamal Abdel Nasser, the Egyptian military strongman, was seen as a twentieth-century Saddam who could help integrate the fragmented Arab world. His efforts at integration, this Arab school of thought would argue, was stymied not by Arab unwillingness to unite but rather by the conspiracy between Arab right-wing rulers of the Gulf and the western powers. Working from this perspective, these Arab nationalists found in Saddam Hussein a man of the age who could secure for the Arab world what had been up until now denied them by the former colonial powers from Europe.

The second reaction from the Middle East came from a different group of people. These were Arabs whose center of gravity was determined by their strong fidelity to political Islam. Convinced that the battle in the twentieth and twenty-first centuries would be over which order should prevail, these Arab Muslims see Islam as the final message for mankind and everything should be done by contemporary Muslims to educate the rest of the world about their *Din* (religion). Being convinced about the rightness of their cause and unwilling to accept the rationale given by both the Gulf leaders and the western leaders bent on ousting Saddam Hussein and his armies out of Kuwait, these Muslim Arabs identified in the western media as "Islamic fundamentalists" soon became the most vocal opponents of the western military build-up in Saudi Arabia.

Three things must be said about these "fundamentalist groups." First of all, it should be noted that these groups saw the confrontation between Saddam Hussein and Shaykh Jabbar as a struggle between two undesirables in the Arab and Muslim World. The Shaykh, in the eyes of these fundamentalists, was a ruler who governed his society not in accordance with Islamic law. He was simply a tyrant who draped himself in the raiment of Islam. Unwilling to grant him legitimacy and determined to see the establishment of Islam-oriented political systems in the Arab/Muslim world, these fundamentalists who leaned towards Iraq saw the conflict not of an invader against a victim, but of two powerless Muslim states washing their dirty linens before the glaring eyes of the world and letting their destinies slip into the hands of Western powers. The writings of these fundamentalists argued against the stationing of western troops on the ground because such a decision compromised the territorial integrity of the *Haramain* (holy sites) in the Hejaz province of the Kingdom of Saudi Arabia. It was actually their fear of western design and their uncertainty about the nature of the evolving relationship between the western powers and the Muslim Arab states of the Gulf and the Middle Eastern region that drove them into the arms of Saddam Hussein. Their decision to support Iraq was occasioned by their sympathy for what they perceived as the victim of western conspiracy. Saddam was well-known to these fundamentalists because many of their fellow activists in the Republic of Iraq were massacred by the secret police of Saddam Hussein or forced to flee for their lives abroad.

To say that these fundamentalists were ignorant of Saddam's excesses is to deny logic to them. What we can say is that they saw the Gulf crisis in a different light. Whereas citizens and leaders of the Gulf countries viewed events after August 2, 1990 as the unfolding of disastrous policies from Saddam Hussein and his cohorts, these fundamentalists took a different line of argument. They told the world, in their diverse publications, that the road to any meaningful peace in the Middle East was to tackle the Zionist menace and to keep western interlopers from penetrating their countries. To these Muslim Arab fundamentalists, the Gulf crisis was a trial, a *fitna*, to test the spirit of the Muslims. After having received the *baraka* (blessings) of Allah through the huge profits made from the sale of petroleum in the 1970s and 1980s, Gulf Arab Muslims were expected to celebrate the praises of Allah for being very generous to them. Instead of doing so, the fundamentalists argue, these men and women of the region have squandered their wealth in the West and have done nothing significant for their less fortunate Arab and Muslim brethren. It was indeed against this background that Sunni fundamentalists in the Arab and Muslim world echoed the same words that have reverberated in the firmaments of Muslim political debates since the eruption of the Iran revolution.

It should be pointed out here that, during and since the Iran revolution, many people in the Islamic movement have come to accept the claim that the oil-rich Muslim states of the Middle East have been very selfish in their appropriation of wealth and in the conduct of their diplomatic relations with fellow members of the Organization of the Islamic Conference. This point of view, which ironically was put out by the Iranian revolutionaries in their attempt to drum up support for their cause among the poorer elements in the Muslim world, became a rallying cry for Saddam and his propagandists around the world. Soon the Muslims sympathetic to Saddam began to argue that the struggle was not between an invaded country and an invading country. Rather, they told us, what was at stake was the collective wealth of the Muslim world. This wealth which has been squandered up to the point of Iraq's invasion of Kuwait, needed to be brought back into the hands of the Muslim peoples of the world. Scarred or scared by this trend of thought among the Saddam propagandists, many leaders of the Gulf countries took the threat seriously and then decided to deal with it frontally.

It was indeed the quick and effective response to these innuendoes and rumor campaigns against the Gulf states that led to the division of opinion among the Muslim fundamentalists. Once the leaders of the religious establishment in the Kingdom of Saudi Arabia, particularly those from the Rabitah al-Alam al-Islami (Muslim World League) and the Darul Ifta, assessed the situation and found that they were being victimized through malicious propaganda out of Baghdad, things began to change for the better. This was evident when leaders from various parts of the Muslim World congregated in Makkah and joined the deliberations on the Gulf crisis initiated by Dr. Abdullah Omar Naseef of the Muslim World League and other Saudi spiritual leaders.

The third group of Arab Muslims who reacted to the Gulf crisis consisted of those Arabs who have now accepted secularism and humanitarianism as two dominant principles in the lives of modern man. Though this group is relatively small in the Arab world, one can argue here that their attitudes towards both Saddam Hussein and Shaykh Jabbar were similar. Much as they regretted the use of force against a sister country by Iraq, they still believed that both rulers were unworthy of their positions and Islam deserved better custodians of the state than what currently existed in both Iraq and Kuwait. To these secular Arab nationalists with liberal political philosophy, the Gulf crisis constituted an opening for the pro-democracy forces in the Middle East. Convinced that the Middle East is the most resistant region on the issue of democratization, and determined to tell the world how things are going in their part of the world, many of the Arab Muslims with secular orientation about politics and the nature of society supported the allied forces not because they welcomed imperial expansion into the Arab/Muslim World, but because they saw a golden opportunity in the restoration of Kuwait and the weakening of repressive regimes like Saddam Hussein.

To these Muslim liberals, the Gulf crisis provided an opportunity for democratization. They actually expressed some republican notions and ideas and looked forward to the day when some semblance of democracy prevails in the Arab/Muslim world. This was certainly the same among certain members of the Kuwaiti resistance. The aftermath of the liberation of Kuwait by the allied forces left no doubt in the minds of the journalists covering the story of Kuwaiti liberation that pro-democracy forces were not pleased with the attempt on the part of the royal family to restore the status quo ante. Convinced that their sacrifices for the restoration of their country's identity and freedom deserve some recognition in the form of constitutional and political guarantees by the ruling family, and determined to enter the twenty-first century by riding on the pro-democratic bandwagon, these Arab Muslim liberals violently opposed the invasion of Kuwait and worked energetically with the various human rights groups around the world. It was indeed their clamor for freedom for the politically repressed elements in the Arab/Muslim world that made a threat to the ruling families of the region and a *bete noire* to Saddam and his cohorts ruling from Baghdad. Though these liberal groups existed long before the invasion, their presence was never acknowledged by the allied powers. The failure to acknowledge them was largely due to the apprehension of the western planners.

Unwilling to open a Pandora's box and determined to link their interest with the collective and individual interest of the Gulf states, the United States of America exercised a great deal of caution on the pro-democracy issue. Various political leaders on the Capitol Hill raised the issue but none made it a do-or-die issue. For this and related reasons, it became categorically clear that the Gulf crisis, like the First World War, was not going to lead to the application by the United States of America of the Wilsonian principle of self-determination, not only in territories where ethnic, religious, and other minorities predominate in the Middle East, but within individual policies where citizens wish to go beyond the right to live within that political system. Retrospectively speaking, one can now argue that the aspirations of the political liberals of the Arab/Muslim world conflicted and still conflicts with the agenda of the ruling groups in the Gulf. In a sense one can draw a parallel between the support given by the Arab Muslim liberals to the joint efforts of allied powers and their Gulf partners and that support which the political liberals gave to the communist rulers of the Soviet Union in the war against the Nazis. Although we share Zbigniew Brezinski's analysis that comparing Saddam Hussein's Iraq to Nazi Germany was incorrect, we can still argue that the political liberals from the Arab/Muslim world of the Middle East entered the war on the side of the monarchs in the hope that democratization would accelerate much faster in affluent kingdoms than in republics of fear.

The last group of Arab Muslims who reacted to the Gulf crisis were those who could best be characterized as the "disillusioned ones." These types were not visible in Arab circles. They usually kept their thoughts secret and shared them only with those who would not betray their privacy and security. Unlike the first three groups, these men and women in the Middle East and beyond feared the fanaticism of the fundamentalists, the idealism of the pan-Arabists and naivete of the political liberals. Cynical to the core and skeptical of those who paraded blueprints for the creation of the new society in the Middle East, these disillusioned ones saw Saddam Hussein for what he really is. To these men and women, he is a dictator who would do everything and anything to have his way. Kuwait, such cynical Arab Muslims would say, was in the way of Saddam and the events of August 2, and after, were the demonstration exercises of Arab machismo. Such daredevil tactics of Saddam Hussein amused them and they recalled quite vividly the good old days of Nasserism in the Arab world. But because these types of Arab Muslims remained inactive throughout the crisis, and since they made little or no effort to jockey for one side or the other, history would not have come to know about their existence were we not fortunate enough to encounter them during the crisis. Their existence, no matter how many they truly number, and their discovery have made us conscious of the various levels of support that are likely to exist in a given society. In assessing the Gulf crisis, one cannot help but ask the question: given the seriousness of the Gulf crisis and the Gulf War, which of the abovementioned reactions really tallied with the majority opinion in the Arab/Muslim world? And how does this opinion relate to the reactions of African Muslims to the crisis. It is to this and other related questions that we now move on to the African continent.

In assessing the reactions of the African states to the Gulf crisis, one must bear in mind that there are two categories of states within the African continent. The first category consists of the North African states that are part of the Arab League and have long-standing links with Arab countries to the east. In the eyes of peoples living in these territories, whatever happens to one part of the Arab world affects the others. Because their history, culture and language are inextricably linked to the Middle Eastern countries, North Africans tend to define themselves and are usually defined as members of the larger Arab world. The second group of countries are the sub-Saharan states that comprise the majority in the Organization of African States. These countries are divided between those with Muslim majority and those with Christian majority. Because of the complex nature of the political, cultural, and historical relationships between North Africans and the sub-Saharan, one encounters varying reactions among sub-Safaran Africans on issues relating to the Middle East. The Arab-Israeli conflict provided a good indication of African opinions on and attitudes towards the Palestinian question. During the Gulf crisis the African states were equally affected by the chain of events in the Gulf region. Surprised at the speed with which the Iraqi army decided to take over the little State of Kuwait and concerned about the implications of the Iraqi invasion for African political stability, many of the sub-Saharan states came out openly and unambiguously against Saddam Hussein and his cohorts in Baghdad. This African stand was motivated by a number of reasons, some of which we intend to explore in the course of this discussion.

But in order to do justice to the subject matter, we must deal with each of the two regions comprising Africa. As we stated above the North African region is closely wedded to the Middle East. On account of these cultural affinities and historical ties, we can begin by saying that three different positions were evident in North Africa at the outbreak of the crisis. The first body of opinion is that of those North Africans who are identified with the ruling classes of the area. These governments were divided between the supporters of Saddam Hussein and those who accepted the mandate of the allied powers and the legitimacy of their mission to dislodge Iraqi military forces from the State of Kuwait. Governments that fall under the first category included the kingdom of Morocco and the United Arab Republic of Egypt. Both of these governments were closely linked to the Gulf states and the western powers. From the Gulf countries both Egypt and Morocco received large sums of money for their developmental efforts. Similarly, both Egypt and Morocco are closely linked to the western donor nations for a number of reasons. Both Arab countries have huge military expenditures and the western countries provide them yearly with allocations and military hardware. Owing to these complex and serious relationships, it was unrealistic to expect the elites of these countries not to go along with the Gulf countries and their western allies. The second category of North African states that lent support to the Iraqi leader and his cohorts were Libya, Sudan, Mauretania, and Algeria.

Though each of these countries had different reasons for rallying around the Iraqis, one could argue that their underlying reason for supporting Iraq was their reluctance to be bedfellows with western powers that were perceived to be imperialistic and arrogant. The Libyans had their own bout with Washington during the second term of President Reagan. They had also crossed swords with the British and the French. Because of their own defiance of western political and cultural hegemony, the Libyans saw the Iraqis going through the same kind of treatment that they went through during the Reagan years in the White House. Unnerved by their past experiences and unwilling to appear as cowed into submission by the European and American forces, Qaddaffi and his comrades saw the Gulf Crisis as another challenge to Arab honor and dignity. In the absence of any other evidence, one cannot argue otherwise. The Sudanese decision to go along with Saddam Hussein must be understood in terms of Sudanese politics and the military, political, and strategic considerations of the Islamic fundamentalist regime in power. Hemmed in by the forces opposed to their fundamentalist prescriptions for Sudan and determined to survive at all costs, the rulers of Sudan decided to join the Iraqi bandwagon because the Fertile Crescent state has been a strong supporter of their cause, even though the Baathist regime headed by Saddam Hussein has been known to liquidate members of fundamentalist groups in Iraq. Actually, when we look retrospectively at the situation in the region and the emerging pattern of political alliance during the Gulf crisis, it becomes quite evident that what motivated the Sudanese leadership was political interest and political survival through Iraqi assistance. The same kind of arguments can be put forth when examining the evidences about Mauretanian policy towards the Gulf crisis. In the case of this Northwest African state, one can make the point that the leadership benefitted a great deal from Iraqi financial and military assistance. This was most evident during the border crisis between the Senegalese and the Mauretanian governments. Committed to Arab nationalism and unwilling to come to terms with forces that are opposed to it, the Mauretanian government found in Saddam Hussein a distant cousin who was willing to play benefactor and arms provider.

When we look at the case of Algerians, we find that they supported Saddam Hussein because of their domestic situation. Faced with a growing movement agitating for an Islamic state, and widely identified with the pan-Arab cause, the leadership in Algeria found itself in a difficult political dilemma. Deciding to take the plunge, these political elites of Algeria found a comfortable middle ground in their expression of opposition to the presence of western forces in Saudi Arabia. By doing so, these shrewd politicos of the Algerian state managed to weather the storm. Retrospectively, one could now argue that the Algerian leaders must have promised themselves the option to change the nature of the relationship between their regime and the Islamic fundamentalist groups.

The recent crackdown on the fundamentalist groups in Algiers and other Algerian towns and cities clearly shows that the Algerian leaders of the FLN were uncomfortable bedfellows with their fundamentalist neighbors during the crisis in the Gulf region of the Middle East.

The Tunisian state's reaction to the Gulf crisis was very similar to what happened in Algeria. Faced with an equally vocal and radical Islamic movement and determined not to be stampeded by these fundamentalists, the government of Ben Ali found in calculated temporary accommodation with the fundamentalists the way out of the crisis. This measure of political expediency bought the regime time to organize for the subsequent showdown with the fundamentalists soon after the end of the Gulf War. Thus, in looking for explanations for the policies of the North African states, especially those of Tunisia, we must remind ourselves that the leaders who had succeeded former President Habib Bourgiba a few years earlier were keenly aware of the dangers to their accomplishments under secular Tunisian nationalism. Unwilling to lose power to the fundamentalists and cognizant of the fact that the PLO headquarters was based in their country, these Tunisian leaders walked the political tightrope with skill throughout the crisis.

When we examine the attitudes of the sub-Saharan African states to the crisis in the Gulf region of the Middle East, we must note the differences of opinions that exist within the membership of the Organization of African Unity (OAU). The African states are not monolithic and, for this and other related reasons, one must always expect a split in their voting on a globally controversial issue. In the case of the Iraqi invasion of Kuwait, none of the sub-Saharan states identified with Iraq. There are several reasons for this unanimity of views within the African camp. First of all, the majority of the African states are tiny entities whose political independence was recognized by the international community through the United Nations. Born under the matronage of the UN system and generally identified as inviable if not absorbable states, many of the small countries in Africa saw themselves as mirror images of the State of Kuwait. If the Iraqis can get away with the invasion and the seizing of their neighbor's lands and riches, many ambitious countries in their neighborhood might begin to have ideas about annexing them. Another reason for the African opposition to the invasion was the general African feeling that Kuwaitis were not bad after all. Since the independence of Africa, Kuwaitis have tried to maintain relations with those African states with whom something mutually beneficial could be worked out. This was the state of affairs with the East African state of Somalia and Kenya; it was much more so in the aftermath of the oil boom of the 1970s when the network of countries dealing with the Kuwaiti kingdom expanded significantly. Many of the African countries that had diplomatic ties with Kuwait did so out of economic and political interest. From the Kuwaiti point of view, such ties as were developed with sub-Saharan Africa proved beneficial and the influence of tiny Kuwait in international circles, particularly the Third World, reached majestic heights.

In addition to the two reasons given above, one could also argue that the African states, especially the predominantly Muslim states, supported the allied actions against Saddam Hussein for political, economic and strategic reasons. The three African states from south of the Sahara to send troops in the Gulf crisis were Senegal, Niger, and Sierra Leone. One may wonder why these three African states decided to send troops to the Middle East. Senegal, we should state categorically, had a vested interest in sending troops. It has been argued in the African media that the decision of Senegal to send troops was a forced one. According to one source, the decision came about when the Senegalese leader found himself in an embarrassing situation soon after a communique was signed by a visiting Senegalese minister and his counterpart in the Beijing government. In that communique an impression was created that Senegal was ambivalent about the Gulf crisis and no strong support for the Kingdom of Saudi Arabia was evident. Disappointed by this poor showing of support for their cause at a crucial period in their history, the Saudi leadership, appreciating the important role of Senegal in African Muslim politics, immediately sought clarification from the Senegalese government.

To allay Saudi fears and determined to prove their loyalty and friendship to the Saudi Kingdom, the government of Senegal decided to go ahead. This decision to send Senegalese troops was not welcomed by the opposition in Senegal. Some of these oppositional forces were sympathetic to the Libyans and the Iraqis. To the Senegalese leadership, however, the decision to send troops was explainable on three levels. At the political level, the Senegalese government could argue that their people have benefitted from Gulf largesse and if a tally of benefits is to be made, not many Africans can claim a greater share of Gulf assistance. On the religious level, the government of President Abdou Diouf could argue that defending the Kaab was a noble cause and African Muslims should not leave the defense of Saudi Arabia to Europeans and Americans. Last but not least, at the moral level, the Senegalese government could argue to its people that the government of Iraq had wronged the Senegalese by providing deadly weapons to the government of Mauretania during the border clashes between their country and neighboring Mauretania. When we look at the case of Niger we find that some of the arguments identified with the Senegalese case can be adduced. Niger belonged to that category of sub-Saharan states that had joined the Organization of the Islamic Conference at the urgings of the late King Faisal of Saudi Arabia. Niger, like Senegal, welcomed the Saudi King in the early 1970s and extended the welcoming mat to many other delegations from the Gulf. Because of her close links to the Saudi Kingdom, not only did she receive Saudi and Gulf largesse but she also enjoyed the benefits of financial assistance from Gulf-dominated international Islamic organizations such as the Islamic Conference and the Islamic Development Bank. While we try to find reasons for the Nigerian decision to send troops to the Gulf, we should point out that the Secretary General of the Organization of Islamic Conference at the time of the Iraqi invasion of the Kingdom of Kuwait was a former Prime Minister of Niger. Taking these facts into account, and bearing in mind that the Saudi leadership needed all the Muslim support it could muster, we can now argue that the Niger contingent was a demonstration of solidarity for the Gulf cause and the OIC Secretary-General acting in a typically Sahelian manner saw in the Nigerian decision to send troops to the Gulf an effective means of reassuring his Saudi co-religionists that they were not fighting alone.

The presence of the Sierra Leonean troops in the Gulf crisis was again motivated by political and economic calculations. Given the record of Saudi-Sierra Leone relations since the 1970s, one could argue that the Sierra Leonean leadership saw in the Gulf crisis an ideal situation to convince the Gulf countries that they were genuine friends and allies and the invasion of Kuwait by Iraq was the ultimate test of their friendship and loyalty. This view has been expressed by many Sierra Leoneans and it is believed the Saudis and their Gulf partners saw the collective African effort as the minimum that these three countries could do to enhance the security of a distant neighbor and a brother in Islam.

In discussing the African reactions to the Gulf crisis we must not forget to state that in addition to Senegal, Nigeria, and Sierra Leone, there are many other African members of the Organization of Islamic Conference. Why did they not participate in the campaign against Iraq? There are several reasons that come to mind. The other predominantly Muslim states that could have participated in the Gulf crisis were barred from participation not because of their limited military prowess but because of their own domestic or regional problems. The largest African state that could have sent a token force in the manner carried out by the three African states identified above was Nigeria. This country that prides itself as "the giant of Africa" is caught in the web of interreligious strife and suspicion. Her leaders who secretly engineered her membership in the Organization of the Islamic Conference were caught flat-footed during the crisis. Unable to respond to any Saudi plea for token and moral support and buffeted here and there by the political winds of domestic forces, the Babangida regime stayed out of the crisis by simply joining the majority of the UN membership in opposing the Iraqi decision to invade Kuwait and in endorsing the use of force to eject the Iraqis out of the State of Kuwait. This decision of the Nigerian government spared the country what could have been a series of violent agitations from the Islamic fundamentalists whose propaganda machine had created the impression that

Nigeria was on the side of the Americans. That political lie which circulated in Nigeria followed an erroneous report in a major American weekly that Nigeria was indeed a part of the coalition forces. This news was quickly challenged by the Nigerian leadership and the damage such an act of disinformation could have had on the Nigerian political scene was immediately reduced. Yet, regardless of how we feel about the Babangida regime in Nigeria, the fact remains that in that country there are sizable number of Islamic fundamentalists who followed the path charted by their spiritual leader Shaykh Ibrahim Yacoub Zakzaky of the Kwarbai Quarters in Zaria City in northern Nigeria.

In assessing the reactions of the African states to the Gulf crisis, one should point out that the African states which did not send forces to fight against Iraq were largely inhibited by their own situation. As stated above, domestic and regional factors mitigated against participation. Let us identify the problems of the main sub-Saharan countries which could not send troops. We have already explained the circumstances facing the Nigerian leadership. Starting from Northwest Africa, one can say that the Republic of the Gambia, a neighbor to Mauretania, an advocate for Iraq, and to Senegal, a party to the allied armada against Iraq, could have joined the Saudis and their Gulf partners in the campaign against Saddam Hussein. Why did they not join the coalition? The answer is that the Gambian Republic was already caught in the delicate negotiations for the resolution of the Liberian crisis. Although the Jawara regime ruling in the Gambia would have liked to send a token force to show their unflagging solidarity with the Saudi Kingdom, the fact remains that a small country like the Gambia is in no position to partake in two military expeditions. The Liberian expedition was a regional campaign against the efforts of Charles Taylor, the guerrilla leader who tried to seize power from the late dictator Samuel Doe. Unable to participate in the Gulf campaign, and determined to be identified with the resolution of the Liberian crisis, the Gambian leaders followed the position which was earlier identified with the government of President Babangida of Nigeria. This policy endorsed the global condemnation of Iraq for her aggression against the State of Kuwait and simultaneously supported the use of force by the allied powers under the auspices of the United Nations. By taking this position, the Gambian government was able to maintain correct diplomatic relationship with the Gulf states. This policy, it must be admitted, was pursued against the background of close diplomatic ties between the Gambia and the Gulf states. Having received from the Gulf countries significant amount of financial assistance over the last fifteen years, and cognizant of the implications of the Iraqi invasion for small states like her, the Gambians found it diplomatic prudential to support the Kuwaitis.

The Republic of Guinea was another African state whose leaders did not bother to send troops to Saudi Arabia. The most obvious reason for the decision not to send troops was the domestic and regional situation for this African state. The government of Guinea found itself in the same situation as the Gambian government. Committed to regional security and cooperation and called upon by the leadership of the Economic Community of West African States (ECOWAS) to participate in the peace-keeping effort in Liberia, the government of Guinea quickly complied. Indeed, we can now say that the domestic economic situation did not warrant a long and distant expedition in the Gulf area of the Middle East. However, viewed from the perspective of Guinean national interest, an expedition closer to home is justifiable because any instability in Liberia could mean trouble as the refugees crossed the common border with Liberia. Added to the fear of mounting refugees crossing the Liberian border was also the fear that many Guinean nationals, especially those that have established residence in this neighboring African state because of trade and commercial ties, would be at risk. To save Guinean and Liberian lives and to strengthen the image of Guinea in African circles, the leadership of this African country stayed away from the Gulf but climbed onboard the African bandwagon to Liberia.

The Republic of Guinea Bissau was another member of the Organization of the Islamic Conference that stayed away from the Gulf expedition. Why did the leaders of Guinea Bissau opt out of the Gulf crisis? The only answer one can ascertain the other sub-Saharan African states, this Portuguese speaking state lacked the means to join neither of the two expeditions begging for volunteers. Guinea Bissau lacked the resources to participate in a distant war and her own immediate national interest dictated a simple endorsement of the global condemnation of Saddam Hussein and the tacit approval of the allied campaign against the Iraqi forces in Kuwait. The lack of resources to assert herself in the council of Muslim states which kept Guinea Bissau out of the Gulf crisis also led to her conspicuous absence from the Liberian crisis.

The Republic of Mali was conspicuously absent in both the Liberian and Gulf expeditions; there is evidence that some limited diplomatic involvement in the attempt to resolve the Liberian crisis took place in Bamako. The diplomats of the now-deposed government of Mousa Traore did join their counterparts working within the framework of the ECOWAS. But in assessing the reactions of the African states to the Gulf crisis, one cannot help saying that Mali was not a leader among African countries in the expression of solidarity with the Gulf kingdoms. Her decision to stay away, it must be emphasized, was dictated by economic problems at home and cautious diplomacy abroad.

The republics of Chad, Cameroon, and Uganda are three other members of the Organization of the Islamic Conference which stayed away from the Gulf War. Why did they stay away and what factors are most likely for their decision not to participate in the campaign against Saddam Hussein? In the case of Chad we can argue that the country simply did not have the resources nor the will to participate in another conflict. Having been ravaged by civil war and a border war with neighboring Libya for many years, and searching for a new lease on life, the Chadian people simply decided to stay home. But while opting not to be part of a wider conflict, they settled for the global condemnation of the Iraqi invasion and accepted the campaign against Saddam Hussein. Although in the midst of the Gulf Crisis a change of government took place in Chad, the successor government did not deviate from the previous government policy by embracing openly and strongly the Saddam Hussein regime in Baghdad. It is true that the international media rumored that Libya had a hand in the coup d'etat against Hissen Habre, the wily fox of Chadian politics; however no convincing evidence contradicted the assumption that the change of government in Chad was occasioned more by personal rivalry than by an external power seeking to install her client in this poor African state.

The Cameroon government may be represented in the councils of the Organization of the Islamic Conference (OIC) but its present leadership under Paul

Biya definitely does not see Islamic solidarity as a priority. Hemmed in by its domestic opponents, and unwilling to bend with the wind of democratic change of the 1990s, the Biya government in Yaounde looked at the Gulf crisis as a distant event. Like its neighbor Nigeria, the Republic of Cameroon also condemned the invasion and expressed support for the allied powers in their campaign against the government of President Saddam Hussein. There are two possible reasons for the Cameroonian expression of support for the Gulf states. First of all, it should be stated that Cameroon did receive Gulf financial assistance in her developmental efforts. Secondly, the involvement of western powers in the Gulf crisis meant that the Biya regime would give full support to their campaign against Iraq.

But if the West African members of the OIC took the positions they did, what factors then motivated the policies of the Ugandan government during the Gulf crisis. Before we probe for the rationale of Ugandan decisions on the Gulf crisis, let us state here that Uganda and Gabon are unique in that they are two non-Muslim majority states that are accepted as members of the OIC. Another point to bear in mind is that President Museveni is a close ally of Libya and the latter has been very critical of the Iraqi invasion and of the stationing of allied forces in the Gulf region of the Middle East. Given the two reasons stated above, one could argue that the government of President Museveni did not rush to the aid of the Gulf states because in the mind of the Ugandan leader, the Gulf crisis was a battle between a struggling Third World country and a western superpower. Yet, following the other African states in the United Nations, Uganda also opposed the invasion of Kuwait by Iraq.

The last member of the OIC to be considered here

is the state of Gabon. This African state certainly earns the distinction of being predominantly Christian and animist (or traditional African) in religion but led by a converted Muslim. A member of the OIC since the 1970s, and sharing membership in OPEC with the Gulf states, Gabon definitely was not an idle stander-by during the Gulf crisis. Motivated by vested interests in oil prices to show concern about what happened to Kuwait, and conscious of the fact that she too has powerful neighbors who might carry out the same scheme as the Iraqis, the Gabonese leaders most probably found the decision of the United Nations Security Council quite effective. In assessing African opinions on and attitudes towards the war in the Gulf, we can only say that Gabon and Nigeria were the only sub-Saharan states that had direct financial and political interests in the resolution of the conflict. Like Nigeria which drew a handsome amount from the sale of her oil during the embargo on Iraq and the total collapse of the Kuwaiti oil industry. Gabon also benefitted from the sale of her oil during the embargo on Iraq and the total collapse of the Kuwaiti oil industry, Gabon also benefitted from the sale of her oil resources. Again, like Nigeria, Gabon endorsed the UN resolutions condemning the Iraqi invasion and supported unreservedly the use of military actions against President Saddam Hussein.

But after having said all these things about the African states that are members of the OIC, let us now look at the policies of the non-Muslim states in the continent. The seven large states whose policies on the Gulf crisis deserve our attention consist of the following: Ghana, Cote Ivoire, Zaire, Zambia, Ethiopia, Tanzania, and Kenya. Ghana has a minority Muslim population that is never visible in that country's political life.

Though the situation has improved for the Muslims in that part of Africa, there is evidence to show that Islam does not have much impact on public policy. Because of this and other related reasons, one could argue that the policy of the regime in Accra during the Gulf crisis was motivated more by expediency than by any other consideration. Like Nigeria and the other African states involved in Liberia's crisis, Ghana had troops in Liberia almost around the same time that U.S. and allied troops were massing against Saddam Hussein and his forces. Because of her involvement in Liberia, Ghana did not bother to entertain the idea of taking sides in the Gulf War. Although President Rawlings is believed to be close to the Libyan leader, Muammar Qaddaffi, there is no evidence from the Ghanaian side to demonstrate any Libyan success in rallying this West African state to the side of the opposition to allied forces in the Gulf. Like Nigeria, Ghana too took the easy way out in the crisis by supporting UN resolutions attacking Iraq for her invasion of Kuwait. This policy kept Ghana within the circle of international diplomatic respectability without necessarily jeopardizing her image as a member of the Third World radical countries.

Cote Ivoire is another country whose policies during the Gulf crisis warrant our attention. Before we proceed with the analysis of Ivoirian motives and interests during the crisis and the war, we should point out that this African country was a member of the Security Council during the crisis. This position within the United Nations system put her diplomats at the center of world diplomacy at a crucial time in world history. How did the Ivoirian leadership respond to the global call for action against Iraq? Based on the available evidence, we can safely state here that the government of Cote Ivoire was among the strongest opponents of the Saddam at the Security Council. Unlike Cuba and Yemen, which supported all the way the Iraqi position, Cote Ivoire sided with the western powers and helped in delivering the necessary votes at the right times.

Zaire is another African country with a small Muslim population. Her policy towards the Gulf crisis is therefore not motivated by Islamic solidarity. Rather, her policy on the Gulf crisis was the result of political calculations made by her shrewd leader, President Mobutu Sese Seko. Closely tied to the West and having reconciled with the Israelis since his decision to re-establish diplomatic relations with the Jewish state, President Mobutu saw in the Gulf crisis a dangerous situation. As a result of these calculations, the Zarois leader joined the rest of the world in their condemnation of the invasion of Kuwait and in their call for the use of military action to push the Iraqi forces out of Kuwait.

The Ethiopian state was caught in the web of internal breakdown during the Gulf crisis. Although the Mungestu regime was at one time aligned with the governments of Iraq, Yemen, and Libya, by the time of the Gulf crisis those bonds had weakened. Over the last two to three years, the desperation of the Ethiopian government forced its leaders to strike a bargain with Israel. This rapproachment with the Jewish state created formidable enemies for Ethiopia and her leaders. When the Iraqis invaded Kuwait, the government joined the other countries at the United Nations to denounce the invasion. As a member of the Security Council, Ethiopia joined the allied powers in their call for action against Iraq. Much has been said about this policy of the Ethiopian government at the time. However, in retrospect, one can argue that the Ethiopians were hemmed in and so could not do anything. Dependent on western countries for food for their starving millions, and caught in the midst of a raging civil war, Ethiopia was a country whose will had been broken and whose energies wasted on the altar of ethnic and regional egoism.

The government of Kenya was another African regime whose policies at the time of the crisis should be examined. Three reasons can be presented for consideration. The first was strategic; the second, political; and the third, economic. The strategic reason for Kenya's decision to support the western powers was self-evident to the Kenyan leaders. Receiving a handsome sum of money from the United States every year for the naval facilities which enable U.S. ships to ply the Indian Ocean, and concerned about the infiltration of the Indian Ocean region by politically radical forces from areas farther to the north or east, the ruling party of President Arap Moi found the best solution to the Gulf crisis in his decision to work very closely with the allied powers. The political reason for the government in Kenya to support the condemnation of Saddam Hussein and the undertaking of military actions against his country, was the desire to respond favorably to the calls for support from the Gulf countries. Kenya, it should be pointed out, is one of the eastern African countries whose nationals travelled to the Gulf region for employment in large numbers. And most of those who journeyed to that region do claim some genealogical links with the peoples of that part of the Arab world. Because of this and other related reasons, the Kenya government found it politically prudent to demonstrate her support to the Gulf countries.

8

SAUDI ARABIA AND THE MUSLIM WORLD

In our discussion of the Gulf War, we have dealt with a number of important issues which have direct or indirect social and political forces in the Saudi Kingdom. In this section of the book, we intend to discuss the relationship between Saudi Arabia and the Muslim world. Saudi Arabia, it should be noted, is unique among the Muslim states because it is the homeland of the Holy Prophet Muhammad and harbors two of the three most important shrines of Islam. Because of this unique place and role in the Muslim Ummah, its relations with other Muslim states, especially at a critical period in her life such as the Gulf War, deserves some examination.

This chapter is divided into three sections. The first deals with the role and place of Saudi Arabia in the Muslim world; the second looks at her role in the Muslim world after the Gulf War; and finally, the third section addresses the impact of the Gulf War on the political situation in the Kingdom of Saudi Arabia. The underlying assumption in all these sections is that Islam is a potent factor in Saudi Arabia and the Saudi leadership has been able to use its potency not only to mobilize and galvanize its citizens but to draw upon the wells of emotional support scattered around the Muslim world. Added to the above-mentioned assumption about the role and place of Islam in Saudi foreign policy, is our recognition that the rivalry between pan-Arabism and pan-Islamism has been fought most vigorously between Saudi Arabia and Egypt under Nasser. Thus, while examining this history of Saudi foreign relations with the Muslim world, we will pay attention to the past events which have direct bearing on the subject at hand.

A. The Kingdom as Protector of Holy Sites

The Kingdom of Saudi Arabia's reputation and status in the Muslim world does not rest only on the petro-dollar. Opponents of Saudi Arabia in the international community have dwelled heavily on what they called "Saudi petro-dollar diplomacy." Those who peddled this anti Saudi propaganda in the international community are usually more secular-oriented than those who see the real basis of Saudi influence among Muslim countries. To Muslims, as opposed to secular-minded members of the international community, Saudi Arabia is famous for five important reasons. First of all, Islamic history began in Arabia, although Muslim theologians and scholars would immediately correct you by saying that Islam with a capital I certainly goes back to the Prophet Muhammad, but Islam with a small i was here in this world since the days of Adam. It is on account of this theological understanding that the Muslim sees Saudi Arabia as the place where the last of all prophets appeared. Hence the Prophet is called *Khatim-nabiin* (seal of the prophets). Muslims who go for the *hajj* (Islamic pilgrimage) see their visit to the Arabian Peninsula as a re-enactment of the life and times of the Prophet. This second reason is taken seriously by the

Muslims and it is responsible for the millions of pilgrims flocking to Makkah and Medinah every year. The third reason why Arabia is sacred to Muslims is because Prophet Ibrahim (known as Abraham to Christians and Jews) spent part of his life in that part of the world. According to both the Quran and Muslim legends, Ibrahim came to the place where the city of Makkah now stands and set up the *Kaaba* (the famous Black Stone to the westerners). Muslim pilgrims re-enact the life and times of Prophet Ibrahim and that of his Egyptian wife Hagar when they performed the *ummah* and the *hajj*. During the *ummah* the Muslim pilgrim circumambulates the Kaaba seven times in memory of the acts of submission to Allah by Prophet Ibrahim, following the successful completion of this most sacred of places of worship for the Muslim. After performing the *tawwaf* (circumambulation around the Kaaba), the Muslim pilgrim is expected to make two *rakas* (a complete series of genuflections and prostrations before Allah), he or she re-enacts the historical event which dramatizes the frantic search for water by Hangar, after Prophet Ibrahim left her alone with young Ismael in the Arabian wilderness. This story of Prophet Ibrahim and Hagar parallels the Biblical account. Muslims believe that through their annual event of the *hajj* they are actually renewing the historical links between the Abrahamic message of monotheism and the final revelation delivered to mankind by Prophet Muhammad of Makkah. Owing to these deep and emotionally charged connections, it is understandable how and why Muslims are very disturbed about the likelihood of this priceless piece of real estate to fall into the hands of non-Muslims. Related to the re-enactment of the life and times of Prophet Ibrahim is the story of Prophet Ismael, the father of the Arabs and the son of Hagar.

One of the most important acts of the *hajj* is the offering of sacrifices. This act of worship takes place at Mina, a distance of about five miles outside of the city limits of Makkah. Both the Qur'anic and Biblical accounts described how Prophet Ibrahim was tested by God (Allah) to offer his son as sacrifice. The ending in both stories is similar in that the object of sacrifice was spared the knife when Allah decided to acknowledge the faith of Ibrahim by sending him a ram to be sacrificed in place of his son. To commemorate this miraculous act of mercy on the part of the Creator, Muslim pilgrims followed the footsteps of Prophet Ibrahim by offering an animal sacrifice at Mina. Another important act of worship for the Muslim pilgrim relates to the temptation of Prophet Ibrahim by the devil (Satan). To celebrate the triumph of Prophet Ibrahim over the devil, the Muslim pilgrims engage annually in ritualistic stonethrowing against Satan at a place called Jamra. These acts of worship performed by the pilgrim during the period of *hajj* are very important to the Muslim world and for this and other related reasons, the Kingdom of Saudi Arabia is very strategic to them. The fourth reason why Saudi Arabia is important to the Muslim world is that many of the historically celebrated leaders of the different groups of Muslims around the world have at one time or the other visited the holy places and in the countless stories and legends about them the holy places are prominently featured. Those who follow these religious leaders look with yearning to travel to the holy places and re-enact during their own lifetimes the experiences of their spiritual masters and mentors. A good indication of the importance of Saudi Arabia to the masses in the Muslim World is the hundreds if not thousands of songs about Makkah and Medinah in hundreds of languages spoken by Muslims around the world. This phenomenon is beginning to be registered even in the western world where there is now a growing number of people who identify with Islam and are adding to the growing body of Islamic literature from the modern western world. The fifth reason why Saudi Arabia is important to Muslims around the world and is of strategic significance in the council of Muslim states is her petro-dollar status within the Organization of Petroleum Exporting Countries (OPEC). With more than a quarter of the world's reserve of oil, and being home to a population that is less than ten million, Saudi affluence is guaranteed for the foreseeable future. Because of this fantastic wealth many Muslims believe that the wealth is a gift from Allah to both the inhabitants of that peninsula and to the larger Muslim world. They argue that Saudi leaders must not only use the resources wisely but they must make sure that affluence does not lead to the deterioration of moral standards within the Kingdom. Any lapse in moral standards has profound repercussions in the Muslim world because annually Muslims journey from various points on the globe to perform the *hajj*. Given these realities, they argue, it is dangerous and unwise for the Saudi leadership to let the expanding global consumeristic culture to envelop their society and thereby weaken the spirit of Islamic culture in their society. This is most forcibly argued by Africans, Pakistanis, Indians, and Malaysians. Echoes of this concern are also coming nowadays from the western Muslims of the Americas, Europe, and Australia.

It is indeed against this background that one can study Saudi foreign policy in the Muslim world. In order to do justice to the analysis of Saudi foreign relations with the Muslim World, the analyst must take into account four variables which are critical in terms of

Saudi policy. The first is the national interest of Saudi Arabia as defined by the ruling family. The national interest of any country can be analyzed either in terms of the realist school as represented by the writings of Hans Morgenthau or in terms of the idealist school which focuses more on the ideological engine propelling the ship of state of a given country. According to the realist school, the Saudi ship of state is navigating dangerous waters and its leadership has very limited latitude in not doing what is in the best interest of those onboard the ship of state. Like a person in a straitjacket the leaders of a country, in this case Saudi Arabia, must act in a certain way to advance their country's national interest. If this point of view is accepted, then it comes as no surprise that the foreign policy of Saudi Arabia is driven by the dynastic interest of the ruling family rather than the faithful implementation of an Islamic doctrine of Muslim solidarity, a point of view most likely to come from an idealist theory of international relations. Given these two competing perspectives on international relations of countries, it is our contention in this chapter that the history of Saudi relations with the countries of the Muslim world demonstrates that both the realist and idealist perspectives exercised some influence at one time or the other.

The second variable in the conduct of Saudi foreign relations is the political environment in which the Saudi leadership operates. Forced to live in a volatile and unpredictable neighborhood, and determined to survive at all costs, the Saudi leadership has done everything within its power to flow with the stream of history in both its neighborhood and in the wider world. The environment in which Saudi Arabia lives is beyond the control of the Saudi leadership; however, occasionally the Saudi leaders manage to influence the course of events by employing certain strategies which make them a part of a winning coalition or a successful defense mechanism to contain the onslaught of aggressive forces in their neighborhood. The environment in which the Saudi leaders have found themselves since the establishment of the kingdom under King Abdul Aziz Ibn Saud, has changed from colonial to Arab socialist to Islamically fundamentalistic and many other things in between.

The third variable in the diplomatic universe of Saudi foreign policy is the personality of the Saudi King and the directions he charts for his country. Since the time of King Abdul Aziz, five members of the al-Saud family have mounted the throne successively. Each of these five men is different from his successor or predecessor. The first King in this century was basically a man of the desert and he ruled the Kingdom much like his ancestors who lived in the Arabian desert. His familiarity with the world beyond his tent was informed to a certain degree. But on the whole it was limited and he never ventured beyond the familiar grounds of his Kingdom. This was not the case with his children who followed him in steady succession. King Saud ruled for about eight years and throughout this period, he showed his passion to travel abroad in grand style. His successor was the more prudential and sagacious King Faisal. Ascending the throne against the background of popular and ulemaic outcry against his brother's excesses, the new Saudi King made sure that life under his leadership was not only better but more impressive in Muslim eyes abroad. This record of King Faisal was maintained but not surpassed or even measured up to by the quiet and non-charismatic King Khalid. The death of King Khalid opened the way for King Fahd whose elevation was widely anticipated by the modernist forces in Saudi

Arabia. The present king has a style of leadership and public relations which is different from both his father and his brothers Faisal and Khalid. Unlike his father who was deeply rooted in the world of the Bedouin, King Fahd is a cosmopolitan member of a royalty whose younger members arc increasingly absorbed in the global culture of consumerism and international finance.

The fourth variable in the conduct of Saudi foreign policy in the Muslim world is the changing Muslim opinions on and attitudes towards the Kingdom of Saudi Arabia. This variable is significant because Saudi Arabia lives within five concentric circles: the Gulf, the Arab, the Muslim, the Third Word and the Global. Each of these circles demands some attention from the Saudi foreign policy makers and the reactions from the Saudi leadership is determined in many instances by a combination of the other three variables identified above. Thus when we analyze the foreign policy of Saudi Arabia towards the Muslim world we must take note of the fact that policymakers in that country *do* pay attention to their image among Muslims because the only credible constituency they have is the Muslim world. Of the five concentric circles, three consist of fellow Arabs, fellow Muslims, and fellow Third Worlders who see in the Kingdom a potential success story in the difficult journey to industrialization.

Taking these variables into account, let us now examine historically the relations between the Kingdom of Saudi Arabia and the Muslim world. When the late King Abdul Aziz came to the throne over seventy years ago, the geopolitical arena called the Middle East had already witnessed the collapse and dismemberment of the Ottoman Empire. Living in a world where European powers have reduced much of the world to colonial fiefdoms, and the Arab world in particular to colonial or mandated territories, the Saudi leaders worked out a modus vivendi with the superpowers of the day. Here the British were particularly important because their political and military might allowed them the opportunity to control Iraq, Transjordan, Egypt, and farther afield, colonial India. Each of these countries had sizeable Muslim population whose religion tied them to the Saudi Kingdom. Though limited in both military and political power, the Saudi leaders survived the colonial period in their neighborhood by staying clear of the path of the competing political forces. During this period, a number of events took place in the neighborhood and within the Muslim world. There was the famous Khalifa movement in the Indian subcontinent. This protest against the abolition of the caliphate by the government of Ataturk of Turkey did not receive support from the Saudi King who could have capitalized on the movement and made a bid for the leadership of the Muslim world. Throughout his rule King Abdul Aziz asserted the territorial integrity of his kingdom and constantly reminded Muslims from abroad that policies regarding the holy sites rested exclusively in his hands. This was made categorically clear during the interwar period when foreign Muslims, especially those from British India, tried to argue for the internationalization of the holy cities of Makkah and Medinah, a demand which would later surface in Libya where Muammar Qaddaffi reiterated the call during the Gulf crisis. What needs to be borne in mind at this time is that the Saudi leadership under King Abdul Aziz was able to survive the challenges to its existence from the colonial and anti-colonial forces because it stayed away from their path. By maintaining correct relations with the British and other European powers in the area, and by avoiding any serious and complicated entanglements with the anti-colonial forces of the Muslim world, the Saudi leaders made their way to the post-colonial period. But as soon as they entered the postwar period, the environment changed from colonial to post colonial. This transformation which was the result of nationalist agitation among the peoples of the Middle East soon began to impact on the Saudi political system. The first volley directed against the ruling family came out of Egypt where the Free Officers under Gamal Abdel Nasser had seized power from King Farouk, a rival to the Hashemite and up until his overthrow an ally of the Saudi dynasty. This revolutionary group of military men created a new environment which did not only threaten the ruling House of Saud but all other monarchies in the neighborhood. Because of this combination of a revolutionary environment dominated by the Cold War and what the late Malcolm Kerr called "the Arab Cold War," the Saudi leadership found itself challenged and vilified. A war of words soon erupted between Cairo and Riyadh and this propagandistic vituperation gradually dragged new combatants from the area. In order to fight back the pan-Arabists, the leaders of the Kingdom began to seek allies within the Arab and Muslim world. The first batch of friends and allies were the members of the Muslim Brotherhood of Egypt fleeing from the politics of repression. These men and women were recruited to give services to the embattled kingdom during the reign of King Saud. However, they would be most effectively deployed when King Faisal took over the leadership of the Kingdom at this critical juncture when the forces of Arab nationalism posed a formidable threat to the Saud dynasty. Determined to save his father's kingdom and to reassert the position of Islam in the Arab and Muslim world, King Faisal took a number of decisions which later helped consolidate his kingdom and enhance the power and prestige of the ruling family. The first order of business for him, after the forced abdication of his elder brother King Saud on March 25, 1958, was the establishment of infrastructural facilities and propaganda machines to contain the campaign of lies and calumnies hurled at his family by the Nasserites operating out of Egypt. To realize his objectives he deployed many of the non-Saudi Arab/Muslim supporters in the newly created institutions where the war of words against the Nasserites and the pan-Arabists was being carried out. To this end, he created the Rabitah al-Alam al-Islamia (the Muslim World League), the Islamic University in Medinah and the Voice of Islam, a radio transmitter deliberately set up to counter the Voice of the Arab coming out of Cairo, Egypt. The first organization, which now enjoys the distinction of being the most powerful international Muslim body, was set up purposely to respond to the challenge to Saudi leadership of the Muslim World. In the perception of the Saudi leaders and their friends and supporters in the Muslim world, the Nasserites were making pretence of leading the progressive Muslims by distributing Islamic literature and by giving scholarships to young Muslims from around the Muslim world. These acts of political mischief and chicanery, the argument went, were planned and carried out in the Egyptian Supreme Council on Islamic Affairs (*Majlis*). To ward off such threats from Cairo and to woo and win global Muslim support, the Saudi leaders under King Faisal worked for eight years to counter pan-Arabism with pan-Islamism. This labor of love of the Saudi King, however, did not yield fruits. It was successful later on only because of events unexpected by the Saudis or Muslims from the around the world. It was indeed the provocative act of an Australian Jew who was later dismissed by Israeli authorities as lunatic that set off the chain of events leading to the founding of the Organization of Islamic Conference (OIC) in 1969. At that meeting, it should be noted, the Egyptians were represented. At this time, Anwar Sadat instead of President Nasser occupied the Egyptian seat. It should be pointed out here that this willingness on the part of Nasser's Egypt to attend was occasioned by the humiliating defeat of Nasser during the Six-Day War. The devastation wrought by the Israeli army had sent shock waves around the Arab and Muslim world, and Hassanain Heikel wrote in the *Cairo Documents*, Nasser who was known as the lion of the Arab was reduced to the status of a wounded lion after the June 1967 war. Wounded and demystified as the hero of the Arabs, Nasser and his Egypt soon found themselves in a new environment where Saudi Arabia was increasingly becoming a force to be reckoned with. This point was not lost to President Sadat soon after he took over following President Nasser's death. The new ruler of Egypt reconciled with the Saudi King and Saudi-Egyptian relations began to thaw. King Faisal responded favorably to President Sadat and the two leaders began to change the political landscape significantly in the Middle East. Indeed, the close relationship between King Faisal and President Sadat led many analysts to speculate whether the October war of 1973 was somehow coordinated between the two leaders. The evidence for such a claim has not been brought forth and one can only take it with a grain of salt. However, in the absence of convincing evidence, one can speculate as to the connection between the decision to impose an oil embargo against the West, soon after the October 1973 war. It may well be that the Egyptian leaders felt that they could mobilize public support for the war. And because of their initial success, the masses in the Arab world would take to the streets and pressed their governments to participate in the struggle against Israel. Responding to this environmental climate of opinion, King Faisal decisively threw his lot with the other Arabs who were willing to show their dissatisfaction with the western countries for their lack of concern and interest in the welfare of the Muslim and Arab world. It was as a result of these environmental changes that the Saudi leaders became increasingly leaders in Darul Islam. It was also the period in which the Muslim world began to see greater Saudi aid and financial support for specific projects launched by Muslims and Arabs.

In analyzing the role of Saudi Arabia in international Muslim affairs during the last three years of King Faisal's life, one must pay close attention to the fact that the changing political landscape in the Middle East was beginning to strengthen the hand of the ruling Saudi family. Because of the cautious diplomacy of King Faisal, the kingdom gradually emerged as the dey broker of conflict. This became most evident following the June 1967 war. Between 1968 and 1970, when Gamal Abdel Nasser passed away, the Saudi King enjoyed a great deal of influence. This influence was destined to grow after the oil embargo against the western markets. According to Peter Mansfield's argument in his book, *The New Arabians*, "Faisal's diplomatic skill and unobtrusive firmness immensely increased Saudi Arabia's prestige and influence. Without a trace of flamboyance he had become an international star personality. Among the Arabs his tendency was always towards moderation and conciliation rather than confrontation" (pg.99) Indeed, with the benefit of hindsight, we can argue here that King Faisal's personality and diplomatic skills enabled him to patiently wait his turn to take over the reins of government from his brother Saud and to deal with the Arab republican radicals who waged bitter wars of words and sometimes of blood against him and his fellow members of the ruling dynasty. Prior to his death, he made it categorically clear that he was not fascinated with either of the rival superpowers, although in his day-to-day acts as national leader of Saudi Arabia, he recognized realistically the dependence of his country on the western countries, particularly the United States. But his realistic and pragmatic relationship with Washington did not mean that he toed the line and accepted all or any proposal from that center of power. One issue over which King Faisal was adamant and showed no sign of compromising on was his attitude towards the state of Israel. As far as he was concerned the Zionist menace and the communist menace were two sides of the same coin. Another area where his cautious demeanor and diplomatic tactfulness yielded to other emotions was his reaction to the republican takeover of the government in Yemen. Unlike his reaction to the coup d'etat that swept the Hashemites and Nuri Said out of office in Iraq, the King responded negatively and in a fighting mood to the abolition of monarchy in Yemen. The political and military hostilities that accompanied the military overthrow of the Yemeni ruling dynasty were not quickly brought to an end by King Faisal; rather, he pressed the republicans hard and tried to obtain concessions from Nasser, especially after the June War when the political stocks of the Arab hero plummeted. In both his battle against the Arab radicals and his persistent resistance to the Israeli conquest of Jerusalem and the Palestinian lands, he found in Islam a rallying cry for Arab and Muslim alike. It is indeed this pan-Islamic message of the Saudi King that disappeared with his death. In his younger brother and successor King Khalid, the message called Faisalism continued but not with the self-restrained confidence that radiated from the face of the assassinated Saudi ruler. As fate would have it, the man who played an important role in saving the royal household from extermination in the hands of the Arab radical conspirators fell victim to the treacherous act of a deranged nephew.

From 1975, when King Faisal died at the hands of an assassin, to the present time, the royal family in Saudi Arabia has continued to act in their relations with the Muslim world by employing the principles of Saudi diplomacy laid down by King Faisal. The Saudis are still playing a mediating role in the Arab world. Their skills were tested during the Gulf crisis and it will take some time before the wounds caused by the war to heal. Though they enjoyed much prestige and respect before the war, there is the feeling that Saudi leaders are now too close to the West and this and other related reasons make them less interested in the affairs of the Arab world. Such views about Saudi Arabia are usually the ravings of elements from the extreme left who care little about the fate of the ruling family and the Saudi people. To this group of political animals, the Saudis have too much money and therefore should be asked to cover more and more the expenses of their less fortunate brothers and sisters. Since the rise to power of King Fahd a perception, true or false, has developed about the ruling family. This is the feeling that under Fahd, liberalization of many of the old fashioned practices would be gradually disposed of and a new society would come into being. This new society would not necessarily deviate from the familiar world of Islamic values.

In concluding this section, therefore, it should be pointed out that under King Abdul Aziz, the Saudis faced powerful neighbors in the person of the Sultan at Constantinople and in the various British officers manning the empire from their piece of real estate on the Gulf. The difference between the founding father of modern-day Saudi Arabia and his children after him was that he conquered his territories and was very much at home in the company of the Bedouins he led. His sons found themselves in a new environment not of their making. Those like King Faisal who had travelled extensively saw in Islam and prudential diplomacy the best means of keeping themselves in power. In the particular case of King Fahd, the image of being a progressive prince turned modernizer catches on and many Saudis are somehow optimistic that under his leadership, the Saudis may be able to steer a new course which is a successful combination of the inherited Wahabi tradition and the intellectual and cultural fruits of the modern world. Owing to this assessment of the situation, it is becoming increasingly necessary for the Saudi leadership to work out the best deals with the members of their five concentric circles.

9

CONCLUSION: THE EMERGENCE OF SAUDI ARABIA

Throughout history, wars have proven to be a catalyst for change for victorious nations, both domestically and internationally. In some cases, wars have led to revolutionary transformations on both fronts.

For Saudi Arabia, on the one hand, the Gulf War most definitely will bring important positive changes to the domestic situation, and to its standing in the international community. On the other hand, many will argue that the war did not cause an abrupt alteration in Saudi Arabia's historical course, but rather only accelerated changes that were destined to occur.

At home, the traditional conflict between the Islamic militants and the more liberal business and professional classes has become more pronounced. Fearing that the pro-western tilt would translate into a loosening of the strictly applied Islamic mores from which they derive their authority, the Islamic militants became more aggressive in attacking government policies. Using religious societies, mosques, and bootleg cassette recordings, the militants attacked government decisions to allow stationing of American troops, to support U.S.-

sponsored Middle East peace negotiations with Israel and to borrow $10 billion on the international markets. During the Gulf War, a group of Saudi women staged a protest by engaging in the taboo act of driving their own cars in a suburb of Riyadh. The incident outraged religious conservatives, but was handled deftly by King Fahd.

Both the religious militants and the liberals have been described as vocal fringe groups, relatively small in number, while the majority of Saudis are considered conservative and said to lean more in favor of religious restriction than liberalization.

But the liberals, many of whom are from the business community, insist that the government will have to loosen religious-inspired restrictions on business and social practices if it hopes to create an expanding economic environment capable of meeting the high expectations for opportunity of the emerging generation of young Saudis.

Liberals also complain that militant student groups increasingly are verbally harassing professors and other students that do not share their views. Both sides reportedly are taking advantage of the main Saudi tradition of redress and flooding King Fahd with opposing petitions.

By the end of the 1991, the authorities had turned their attention to the militants, who in their underground cassettes had attacked the Saudi Women's Renaissance Association as "prostitutes" and demanded that it be disbanded. Many of the association's members are also members of the Royal Family. The attack provoked a stern response by Prince Turki al-Faisal, who in a speech at a mosque reportedly warned the Iman that he had gone too far, and that they either must prove their charges or be held accountable for making them. The following week, the Iman admitted his guilt and was fired by his superiors.

This event prompted Sheikh Abd al-Aziz Ibn Baz, the highest ranking religious leader, to announce, "Many of those who pretend to have knowledge and a religious calling," he said, "have in this day and age, surfaced to contest and injure established religious leaders, doing so secretly in their gatherings or proclaiming their views openly in sermons in the mosques, or records these views on cassettes that are distributed among the people. I counsel those who have misguided youths and filled them with hatred and conspiracies and erroneous gossip about such and such person, to repent and desist from those activities."[1]

Several months later, King Fahd issued a long-awaited order for creation of the national consultative council, and for a bill of rights protecting basic individual freedoms such as privacy, and for the first time revising the way the King is chosen. The reforms, which were the product of a pledge the King made in 1978, were designed to expand participation in government decisionmaking. The council, to which the King will appoint sixty members, may slightly favor the business community, as well as the middle class that composes the majority of Saudi society,

Although the reforms did not meet the high standards demanded by some international human rights groups, they were applauded by many foreign governments as important steps toward participatory government and recognition of citizens' rights.

Thus, there was nothing new in the tensions between contrasting wings of the Saudi political spectrum. But the Gulf War certainly intensified competition between them, and accelerated their expression of disagreement. What is new, and yet to be tested, is the legal and administrative framework that the government has created to accommodate their formal participation in its decisionmaking.

Regional Leader

Prior to the Gulf War, Saudi Arabia played a modest role in regional politics, often deferring to its more populous neighbors to take center stage. But the war drastically changed the alignment, knocking out Iraq as a regional superpower and creating a vacuum which Saudi Arabia was obliged to fill.

Although Saudi Arabia and the United States were seen as being the closest of allies, Saudi Arabia did not favor "prepositioning" American troops on the Kingdom's soil. The United States military wanted to "preposition" arms and equipment for 150,000 soldiers on Saudi soil, a policy dream that stemmed from the days when pro-Israel hawks like Richard Perle and Stephen Bryen were prominent in the Pentagon.

The United States' push for a "forward headquarters element" in the Kingdom was particularly insensitive, considering that the two sides agreed explicitly at the outset that U.S. troops would leave when the job was finished, and that there was widespread domestic and regional opposition to a continued foreign military presence. What the Saudis naturally wanted was to build up its ground forces so it would no longer be dependent on foreigners for its defense. The Defense Department and the State Department tried to use this as leverage to persuade the Saudis to agree to a new defense cooperative agreement, much like the one Kuwait signed with the U.S. In particular, the State Department indicated that it did not want to sell arms that the Saudi buildup entailed at a time when it was supposed to reduce arms sales in the Middle East.

The Saudis were probably not encouraged by the fact that two of the American officials pushing the prepositioning plan were Defense Undersecretary Paul D. Wolfowitz and Assistant Secretary Richard Clarke, both known for being pro-Israeli. Saudi Ambassador Prince Bandar Ibn Sultan repeatedly rebuffed requests for meetings from Clarke, who subsequently was implicated in a State Department Inspector General report on unauthorized transfers of U.S. technology to Israel.[2] The State Department even moved to reprimand Clarke.[3]

In an ambiguous compromise, the United States and Saudi Arabia in May 1992 settled on an obscure fifteen year-old military training pact as the legal framework for a broad expansion of strategic cooperation between the two nations, according to the American and Saudi officials interviewed by the *Washington Post*. Known as the 1977 Military Training Mission Treaty, the accord was invoked to justify the stationing of a small number of military advisers in the Gulf region, including Saudi Arabia, as well as storage of support equipment for five or six fighter wings (400 planes) and some tanks and fighting vehicles. The scale of the storage operation is only a fraction of the original prepositioning plan proposed by the Pentagon. Moreover, many details were left for negotiations which promised to drag on well beyond the November 1992 U.S. presidential election, as the Saudis wanted to await the results of those elections before proceeding. The Saudis reportedly made it clear that in no way should the agreement suggest acceptance of a permanent U.S. military base.[4]

On the issue of Iraq, the Saudis were aggressively pressing the United States to carry out a covert action campaign to topple Saddam Hussein. The initiative, according to the *New York Times*, sought an allied effort to supply arms and intelligence to Kurdish rebels in northern Iraq, Shiite Muslim fighters in the south and Sunni Muslim opposition forces in central Iraq. The aim was to draw and divide Saddam Hussein's last Republican Guard divisions protecting his strongholds around Baghdad and subject them to allied air assaults. The plan, which sounded more like a psychological warfare game out of the CIA's "Bay of Pigs Institute for Success Overseas" than a serious operation, apparently was never carried out.[5]

Instead a report surfaced in May 1992 that the CIA was flooding Iraq with counterfeit currency in an attempt to destabilize the government. However, the *New York Times* reported there was no evidence the operation was effecting any real progress towards overthrowing Saddam. The *Times* also reported that the Bush Administration authorized full-fledged covert operations against Iraq in February 1992.[6] While the Saudis undoubtedly benefitted from the close military alliance with the United States during the Gulf War and were impressed by American prowess, they are likely to learn that the successes of CIA covert operations are fewer and farther between.

Saudi-Iranian Competition

While much attention remained on Iraq, the two main competitors for regional influence were Saudi Arabia and Iran. This was an age-old competition, dating back to the origins of the split between Sunni and Shiite Muslims a millennia ago. Iran continues to seek to export is style of Islam, and has the manpower, military equipment, and ten years of experience in its favor. Iran's main weakness is its anemic economy and risk of growing internal dissension caused by scarcity and dissatisfaction with the ruling Mullahs.

Another factor intensifying the competition was the break up of the Soviet Union and the quest to be the main Islamic ally of the former Soviet republics of Azerbaijan, Kazakhstan, Kirghizia, Tajikistan, Turkmenistan, and Uzbekistan. Only Azerbaijan was Shiite, while the other were Sunni. Iran has tried emphasizing cultural and religious connections, particularly to Azerbaijan, but has run into stiff competition from Turkey, which in fact has stronger historical and cultural ties with the region, and appeared to be cooperating with Saudi Arabia.

In Sudan, Iran appears to have more success applying a formula it used in Lebanon to maximize its influence: supplying Revolutionary Guards, intelligence training and arms to a strong Islamic fundamentalist leader, Sheik Hassan al-Tourabi.[7] Al-Tourabi has used the support to consolidate power and stamp out a rebellion by the Sudan People's Liberation Army, which represented the southern, predominantly non-Muslim southern region of Sudan.[8]

As Eabal Ahmad wrote, "The Saudis were quick to counter Iran's proselytizing zeal and were generously supported in this by Kuwait and other Gulf emirates. Islamic activists and organizations around the world became beholden to one or the other of the two centers of Islamic politics. During the Iran-Iraq War, secular Iraq joined the religious crusade. The Iran-Saudi Arabia divide came to be reflected in nearly all Islamic political parties worldwide. The opposing camps had violent encounters in places such as Afghanistan, Pakistan, and Lebanon, even before the Persian Gulf war."[9]

Iran has sent money and "cultural attaches" to countries as distant as Ghana and Nigeria, Muslim students from Thailand, Burma, and Indonesia receive scholarships to study in the Iranian city of Qum.[10]

In October 1991, the Iranian Parliament sponsored a conference in Tehran to discuss ways of assisting the Palestinian Intifadeh and to "Islamicize" all opposition in Israel.

Iran's ambitious designs on regional leadership could be hampered -- and ultimately aborted -- by internal discontent spawned by a worsening economy and continued oppression of individual freedom. Iranians in the Azerbaijan region reportedly were assassinating Revolutionary Guards on mountain roads at night.[11] In May 1992, the *New York Times* reported the latest in a series of violent inner city riots by poor Iranians who responded to attempts by the authorities to evict them from public land.[12]

Some observers have speculated that the nuclear arena could emerge as another area of competition between the two Islamic regimes. CIA Director Robert M. Gates told Congress that Iran is trying to acquire a nuclear weapons capability, but predicted that this goal was unlikely to be achieved before the year 2000. While Iran officially denied seeking the bomb, some Iranian leaders publicly proclaimed that they would have the first "Islamic" nuclear weapon.

A likely resource for any Mideast nuclear program (aside from Israel's) is the Iraqi nuclear program. The main strength of the Iraqi program was the estimated 4,000 Arabs, many of them Palestinians and Egyptians, who arrived in Baghdad between 1974 and 1977, to work on the Saddam's nuclear effort. These engineers and scientists were responding not only to promises of higher pay, but also to the appeal of working in an all-Arab program. One of the leading Iraqi nuclear scientist, Hussein Sharistani, a Shiite, claimed he refused to work on the program when he discovered it was designed to build a bomb. He was arrested in 1979 and tortured and charged with membership in an anti-regime organization. He was sentenced to twenty years in prison but escaped to Iran in 1991 after an allied air raid on Abu Ghraib prison in Baghdad.

The end of the Gulf War led to revelations that shocked the world into realizing how close the Iraqis were to developing the bomb. Is it far-fetched then to speculate that the these revelations sparked an intense competition between Iran and Saudi Arabia for the services of these knowledgeable nuclear scientists?

It is worth remembering that the end of World War II set off a similar scramble for Nazi nuclear scientists by two new competitors -- the United States and the Soviet Union -- and ushered in the nuclear age.

Economic Might, Political Power

The Gulf War removed any doubts about Saudi Arabia's ability to convert its oil-based economic wealth into political power. Although the Saudis lacked the military might to counter the Iraqi threat, it assured its own defense by underwriting the biggest, and most complex military buildups in history. It also came through with loans and other financial aid, and persuaded the tight-fisted leaders of Kuwait and the United Arab Emirates to do the same, for key members of the United Nations Security Council, particularly the Soviet Union.

Moreover, the Gulf War forced the traditionally low-key Saudis for the first time to engage in aggressive diplomacy, calling in the favors owed to it by nations throughout the world largely because of the economic relationship. Those like Jordan, which failed to respond as the Saudis expected, paid a high price.

The Saudis have continued a more activist diplomatic role. A prime example came in the precedent-setting Middle East peace conference in Madrid in November 1991. Acting as a personal envoy of King Fahd, Ambassador Prince Bandar was credited with playing a key role in keeping the talks going when it appeared they would collapse. Prior to the historic conference Prince Bandar travelled to Damascus to meet with Syrian President Assad, who assured the prince that Syria would live up to its commitment and attend. But when the three-day opening session of the conference ended in a volley of acrimonious charges and counter-charges between Israel and Syria, Syria was on the verge of bolting without moving on to the vital second stage of direct talks with Israel. Bandar reportedly persuaded the Syrian Foreign Minister to go to the table with the obstinate Israelis. To ensure progress, King Fahd followed up by calling President Assad.

In addition, when the Palestinians and Jordanians said that regardless of Syria's decision, they wanted to proceed to the direct talks with Israel, the Saudis said they would back them in their stand.

During the War, Saudi Arabia helped bring down skyrocketing oil prices by stepping up production to levels few people thought were possible. In the recession that plagued most nations' economies following the war, the Saudis maintained high production levels so as to keep oil prices stable. This stems from the Saudi's "balance of interests" policy which holds that too high of an oil price, though good for short-term windfalls, ultimately will hurt the Saudi economy by dragging down, or even threatening the world economy.

However, when the European Community contemplated altering this balance by a $3 barrel increase in the oil tax, the Saudis flexed their economic muscle. Saudi Oil Minister Hisham Nazir said the tax was designed to finance the EC's own largesse at a time

180

that the twelve EC governments earned $210 billion from oil taxes in 1991. Saudi sources indicated they were willing to limit oil production and let prices rise $3 a barrel. Just the mention of it cause the Dow Jones average to drop twenty-two points, as U.S. dependence on foreign oil was placed at 40 percent. Saudi Arabia, the world's largest oil exporter, provided one of every ten barrels of oil consumed in the United States in 1991.

One important payoff for Saudi Arabia is that it increased its share of the world's oil production from 25 to 35 percent. It continues to diversify it economy through "downstream" oil and petrochemical industries, and through construction. Perhaps the most important result of the post-War order is not that Saudi Arabia has increased its productive capacity, but that it is grappling with the difficult issues of accommodating the needs of its domestic population, while at the same time, learning how to transform its economic might into political influence.

While some experts are predicting that the twenty-first century will belong to Europe, others are saying it will be wise to keep an eye on Saudi Arabia.

---

1. *Asharq Al Awsat,* Dec. 29, 1991.
2. *Washington Post,* Oct. 20, 1991.
3. *Wall Street Journal,* May 5, 1992, pg. 1.
4. *Washington Post,* May 31, 1992, pg. A-10.
5. *New York Times,* Jan. 19, 1992.
6. *New York Times,* May 25, 1992, pg. 1.
7. *New York Times,* Dec. 13, 1991 & May 31, 1992.
8. *New York Times,* June 1, 1992, pg. A-6.
9. *World Press Review,* Nov. 1991.
10. *Time Magazine,* Nov. 4, 1991, pg. 20.

11. Ibid.
12. *New York Times,* June 1, 1992.

182

186

Al- (56)
Nakasone, Prime Minister (106)
Naseef, Dr. Abdullah Omar (133)
Nasser (24),(38),(72),
Nasser, Gamal Abdel (129),(155),
    (163),(165-167)
Nasserite (23),(129)
Nayif, Abdullah al-Razzaq al- (31)
Nazer, Hisham (53),(54),(56)
Nazi (114),(135),(178),(179)
Nebuchadnezzar (7)
Nejd (18)
Nestorian (6)
Nicaraguan (106)
Nidal, Abu (72)
Niger (123),(141),(143)
Nile (1)
Nimrod (5)
Ninevah (5)
Noreiga, Manual (60)
North Sea (54)
OAU (140)
Occupied Territories (51),(105)
OIC (125),(143),(148-150),(165)
OPEC (46),(52-56),(59),(64),
    (150),(158)
Organization of Islamic Conference
    (4),(126),(128),(132),
    (143),(144),(147),(148),
    (165)
Ortega, President Daniel (106)
Osirak Nuclear Reactor (49)
Ottoman Empire (5),(16),(161)
Ottoman Period (4)
Oxus River (7)
Pagonis, Maj. Gen. William (Gus)
    (115-120)
Pakistan (118),(123),(176)
Palestine (21),(24),(103),(105)
Palmyra (9)
Panama (60),(64),(116)
Paris Peace Talks (20)
Parthians (8)
Pentagon (85),(87),(173),(174)
Perle, Richard (173)
Persia (8)
Persian
    (7),(9),(12),(18),(88),(100),(110),
    (119),(176)

Phillipines (118)
PLO (67),(93),(94),(140)
Pollard, Jonathan (85)
Portuguese (17),(18),(147)
Powell, Colin (85)
Primus Inter Pares (12)
Prince Bandar Ibn Sultan (174)
Prince Hassan (102)
Qaddaffi, Maummar (138),(151),
    (162)
Qadisiyah, Battle of (9),(10)
Qasim, President Abdul al-Karim
    (28),(29)
Qatar (56)
Rabat (103
Rabitah al-Alam al-Islami (132),
    (164)
Radio Free Iraq (124)
Rakas (156)
Ramadan, Taha Yasin (33)
Rashid, Harun (13)
Rashid Family of Hail (18)
Rawlings, President (151)
Razzaq, Arif Abdullah al-Razzaq
    (30)
RCC (31),(33-35),(38),(39)
Reagan, President Ronald (138)
Reagan Administration (88)
Red Army (40)
Red Sea (16),(18)
Republican Guard (30),(57),(115),
    (175)
Riyadh (53),(107),(115),(163),(171)
Romans (3),(8)
Roosevelt (114)
Rough Riders (114)
Rumailah (57),(67)
Rumayla (45),(69),(72)
Russians (18)
Saad, Crown Prince (70)
Saad, Sheikh (65)
Saadi, Ali Salih al- (30)
Said, Nuri as- (23)
Sabah, Emir Jaber al-
    (53),(92),(111)
Sabah, Talat Kadrat (106)
Sabic (41)
Sadat,Anwar (165)
Saddam (1),(3),(4),(9),(11),(24),

ABOUT THE AUTHORS

Dr. Sulayman S. Nyang is a Professor of African and Islamic Studies at Howard University, Washington, D.C. From 1986-93, he was chairman of Howard University's African and Islamic Studies Department. A native of Gambia, Dr. Nyang has served as First Secretary and Deputy Head of the Gambia Embassy in Jeddah, Saudi Arabia, has served as consultant to the United Nations in Namibia and has written studies for the World Bank, and the UN Commission on Human Rights in Geneva.

He is the author of *Islam, Christianity and African Identity* (1984) and *Religious Plurality in Africa: Essays in Honor of John Mbiti* (Mouton, 1993). He obtained an M.A. in Public Administration and a doctorate in government from the University of Virginia in Charlottesville.

Evan Hendricks is Editor/Publisher of Privacy Times, a Washington, D.C. newsletter on information law and policy. He has a long-standing interest in Middle East Affairs, and served as a media consultant to the National Association of Arab Americans from 1985-1987.

He is author of *Your Right to Privacy: A Basic Guide to Legal Rights in An Information Society* (Southern Illinois University Press, 1990), and *Former Secrets* (Campaign for Political Rights, 1982). He was editor of *The Armageddon Network* (Amana Books, 1984). Mr. Hendricks graduated with a B.A. from Columbia College, Columbia University. He is a native of Portland, Oregon.